MIND STALKERS

Mind Control of the Masses

By
Commander X
&
Tim R. Swartz

GLOBAL COMMUNICATIONS

Mind Stalkers
Mind Control of the Masses
By Commander X and Tim R. Swartz

Editorial Director: Timothy Green Beckley
Assistant to Publisher: Carol Ann Rodriquez
Editorial Assistants: Sean Casteel, William Kern

Cover Graphics: Tim R. Swartz

Write for our free catalog:

Global Communications
P.O. Box 753
New Brunswick, NJ 08903

www.conspiracyjournal.com

Contents

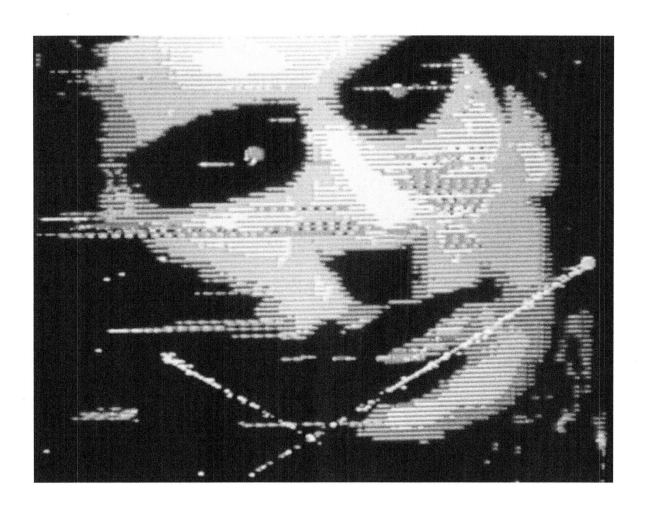

ARE YOU REALLY IN CONTROL?

MIND STALKERS

The dream of every leader, whether a tyrannical despot or a
benign prophet, is to regulate the behavior of his people.

Colin Blakemore

ANIMAL MAGNETISM — The Operator putting his Patient into a Crisis —

The modern practice of hypnosis and mind control can be traced back to Austrian physician Franz Anton Mesmer who developed a technique known as Mesmerism.

MIND STALKERS

INTRODUCTION

The subject of human mind control has long been consigned to the realm of lurid spy novels and grade B action movies. Most people consider the possibility of mind control by outside influences to be nothing more then the ravings of lunatics and psychotics. However, over the years, governments and intelligence agencies have spent millions of dollars in research to determine whether the mind can be regulated, influenced and controlled.

The phrase "mind control" has been defined to mean many different things, and all these definitions have their advocates. Some believe that mind control involves the harassment of individuals for the purpose of disorienting them, or decreasing their ability to discuss issues of importance. This includes the use of less-than-lethal technologies such as microwaves, electromagnetic irradiation, sonic-waves and other techniques.

Other research concerns individual mind control by means of what is called "structured abuse," what L. Ron Hubbard once identified as "drug/pain/hypnosis" conditioning. Discussions on this topic can be found in books and articles related to satanic ritual abuse, alien abductions, and the "false memory syndrome" debate.

This book will examine the history of mind control experimentation, as well as the possible outcome of such research. Some claim that experiments done in the 1940's, 50's and 60's have led to Top Secret electronic machines that are capable of influencing the minds of chosen individuals anywhere in the world.

Others say that microwaves delivering direct-voice communication to the brain are being used to harass American citizens. There is also good evidence suggesting that unwilling victims of sophisticated forms of hypnosis are being secretly programmed to act as assassins when needed.

Because of the outrageous nature of such evidence, the media and the public have been unwilling to consider that their most precious freedom - independent thought - could be seriously compromised.

CHAPTER ONE

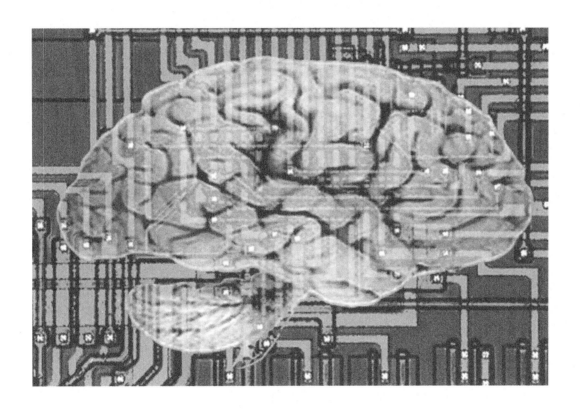

QUEST FOR THE MIND

MIND STALKERS

The Beginnings

Mind control can trace its origins to mankind's distant past with the use of magical rites and Shamanism. Techniques of mind control developed in our western culture are believed to have been field-tested by various mystery religions, secret societies and political organizations.

One of the earliest attempts at mind control involved "Mesmerism," or as it is known today, Hypnotism. Primitive societies have used hypnotic phenomena throughout the ages for physical and spiritual benefits. Tribal drums and ritualistic dances have been a part of many societies worldwide. Believed to have the power to heal, Kings of middle age Europe would touch commoners with remarkable results. Priests and ministers would use a laying on of hands to affect changes in the health and fortune of their church members.

There have even been paintings and sculptures in ancient Greece and Egypt that depict a "curing sleep" induced in subjects by their leaders to affect healing or change of mental attitude. This interesting condition gained the attention of doctors and scientists in the 18th century all because of a man whose name would later become the name of the mental phenomena. That name is Mesmerism.

Considered to be the father of hypnotism, Franz Anton Mesmer was born in Vienna, Austria in 1734. Mesmer in his youth considered first becoming a Priest and then a Lawyer. He finally decided to be a Doctor in Vienna at the age of thirty-two. In 1773 Mesmer, started working with a Jesuit priest by the name of Maximilian Hell, who was also the Royal Astronomer of Vienna, Austria.

The two men treated their patients with magnets and magnetized baths. Hell thought the magnets cured with physical properties, interrupting the sick person's magnetic field. Mesmer thought there was a fluid mineral that pulsated throughout the person's body as well as throughout the universe. He called it "animal magnetism."

Mesmer soon began to experiment with a set of powerful magnets. In one case he softly applied the various magnets to different parts of a female subject. The story claims the woman began to tremble and went into convulsions. Mesmer deduced this was the "crises' state." After a series of such treatments he declared her completely cured.

The "animal magnetism" theory was also confirmed in Mesmer's mind from his personal observation of Father Gassner, who would heal people by using laying on of hands. He would make numerous passes all over the subject's body. Mesmer studied Father Gassner very carefully and theorized that this magnetic fluid circulating in the body was effecting these changes.

Animal magnetism fluid was thought to be affected by forces of energy from astral bodies. There were four primary fluids of concern. These four fluids included blood, phlegm, yellow bile and black bile. Keeping these fluids in harmony was the trick to good health. This theory was widely believed at the time and coincided with Ben Franklin's discovery of electricity and recent advances in astronomy.

Mesmer moved to Paris in 1778 and invented "backquets," large iron pots that could hold a number of adults. Mesmer would line the backquets with iron filings and magnets. Patients would enter the bath, immerse themselves with water and leave cured of their ailment. Mesmer had a very high percentage of cures and members of high society actively sought his services. Many with money to spend would attend the sessions simply for the entertainment.

Mesmer's healing parlors seemed at the time to be more a religious experience then a trip to the physician. The parlor would be a dimly lit, mirror filled room. In the center of the room was a large tub filled with magnetized iron filings and chemicals. Affixed around the edge of the tub were large metal rods protruding outward as handles grasped by a dozen Parisian society ladies and gentlemen. From another room would waft the faint music of a glass harmonica. When the sound trailed off, the door opened revealing a figure complete with an iron rod scepter in one hand and cloaked in a long purple robe.

Those there to be healed would close their eyes in what seemed to be a trance. Some people would report that tingling sensations would run wildly through their bodies. Eventually, the strange feelings would begin to possess the others in the circle. Some would even flail and swoon or go into mild convulsions. Patients were then attended to by assistants who would take them to another room called the "chambre de crises."

In 1784, the French Academy set up a commission to study Mesmer and set forth to find internationally famous scientists to try and explain Mesmer's methods. Ben Franklin from America and Dr. Guillotin, a chemist and inventor of the "guillotine" were among other noted figures asked to study Mesmer and his techniques.

Mesmer took two large iron rods and touched these rods to several trees in the forest to "magnetize" them. His patients were asked to go into the forest and touch the magnetized trees. It was business as usual for Mesmer because many patients came back, cured of their afflictions. However, patients were touching all the trees in the forest, not just the magnetized ones.

Ben Franklin and the other scientists arrived at the conclusion that Messmer was not healing the patients. The patient was healing him/her self by using their own mental power. The patient's imagination was stimulated in such a way that would enable the person to become completely healed. Mesmer was declared a charlatan.

However, as time went by further research on "mesmerism" led many scientists to conclude that Mesmer had indeed accidently discovered a hidden feature of the human mind. A state of mind called "High Suggestibility." Because of this, Franz Anton Mesmer is credited with the discovery of what is now known as hypnosis.

Under The Spell

The history of hypnotism is replete with tales of good people led astray under the spell of an evil hypnotist. The name Svengali has come to mean someone who has an unnatural influence on another, usually with hypnotism. One of the favorite dogmas of modern hypnotism is that "hypnotism can't make a person do anything against his or her moral code."

MIND STALKERS

Some past incidents suggest that certain hypnotists apparently could make some people do whatever they wanted. One such event occurred in 1865 in the French village of Sollies-Farliede. A beggar named Thimotheus Castelan was invited to stay for a night with a man and his adult daughter, Josephine. During the night, Thimotheus hypnotized the woman, then raped and abducted her.

For two weeks the pair kept to the back roads, appearing only for single evenings spent in the homes of other villagers. Thimotheus was seen to make strange signs over Josephine and to mumble instructions. Josephine carried out his every wish.

Finally the authorities caught up with Thimotheus and his unwilling companion. Thimotheus was sentenced to twelve years of hard labor, while Josephine suffered through various nervous afflictions for several months afterwards. The two physicians testified in the case were unanimous in their opinion that the "magnetic effect" destroyed Josephine's moral freedom and her ordinary restraint was lost.

In 1937 a young German woman was hypnotized by a man who falsely claimed he was a doctor. For seven years the woman suffered from various false ailments allegedly induced by the hypnotist. Upon his suggestion she actually murdered her husband believing he was a stranger out to attack her. When the case came to trial, her hypnotically induced suggestions were so complex that it took a court psychiatric consultant nine months to make sense of the situation. The woman was found not guilty. However, the hypnotist managed to escape and was never caught. This case and others like it suggested that mind control was possible.

The Search To Modify Behavior

In mans quest to control the mind and behavior of humans, there was a great breakthrough established by Ivan Pavlov, who devised a way to make dogs salivate on cue. He perfected his conditioning response technique by cutting holes in the cheeks of dogs and measuring the amount they salivated in response to different stimuli. Pavlov verified that "quality, rate and frequency of the salivation changed depending upon the quality, rate and frequency of the stimuli."

MIND STALKERS

Though Pavlov's work falls short of human mind control, it did lay the groundwork for future studies in mind and behavior control of humans. John B. Watson conducted experiments in the United States on a 11-month-old infant. After allowing the infant to establish a rapport with a white rat, Watson began to beat on the floor with an iron bar every time the infant came in contact with the rat.

After a time, the infant made the association between the appearance of the rat and the frightening sound, and began to cry every time the rat came into view. Eventually, the infant developed a fear of any type of small animal. That fear would remain with the infant as it grew up. In a later study conducted on the individual, the irrational fear of small animals was still predominate, even though the individual could no longer remember why.

Watson was the founder of the behaviorist school of psychology. "Give me the baby, and I'll make it climb and use its hands in constructing buildings or stone or wood. I'll make it a thief, a gunman or a dope fiend. The possibilities of shaping in any direction are almost endless.

Even gross differences in anatomical structure limits are far less than you may think. Make him a deaf mute, and I will build you a Helen Keller. Men are built, not born," Watson proclaimed. His psychology did not recognize inner feelings and thoughts as legitimate objects of scientific study, he was only interested in overt behavior.

Though Watson's work was the beginning of mans attempts to control human actions, the real work was done by B.F. Skinner, the high priest of the behaviorists movement. The key to Skinner's work was the idea of operant conditioning, which relied on the notion of reinforcement, all behavior that is learned is rooted in either a positive or negative response to that action.

There are two corollaries of operant conditioning, aversion therapy and desensitization. Aversion therapy uses unpleasant reinforcement to a response that is undesirable. This can take the form of electric shock, exposing the subject to fear producing situations, or the infliction of pain. Aversion therapy has been used as a way of "curing" homosexuality, alcoholism and stuttering.

MIND STALKERS

Desensitization involves forcing the subject to view disturbing images repeatedly until they no longer produce any response, then moving onto more extreme images, and repeating the process over until no anxiety is produced. Eventually, the subject becomes immune to even the most extreme images. This technique is typically used to treat people's phobias. It has been suggested that the violence shown on television could be said to have the unintended effect of desensitization.

Skinners' behaviorism has been accused of attempting to deprive man of his free will, his dignity and his autonomy. It is said to be intolerant of uncertainty in human behavior, and refuses to recognize the private, and the unpredictable. It sees the individual merely as a medical, chemical and a mechanistic entity that has no comprehension of its real interests.

Skinner believed that people are going to be manipulated. "I just want them to be manipulated effectively," he said. He measured his success by the absence of resistance by the person he was manipulating. He thought that his techniques could be perfected to the point that the subject would not even suspect that he was being manipulated.

Mind Control Research Of The Third Reich

At the conclusion of World War Two, American investigators learned that Nazi doctors at the Dachau concentration camp in Germany had been conducting mind control experiments on inmates. They experimented with hypnosis and with the drug mescaline. Though they did not achieve the degree of success they had wanted, the SS interrogators in conjunction with the Dachau doctors were able to extract the most intimate secrets from the prisoners when the inmates were given very high doses of mescaline.

Dachau was filled with Communists, Social Democrats, Jews, Gypsies, clergymen, homosexuals and people critical of the Nazi government. Upon entering Dachau, prisoners lost all legal status, their hair was shaved off, all their possessions confiscated and they were used as slaves for both corporations and the government. As at Dachau, there were fatal mind control experiments conducted at Auschwitz. The experiments there were described by one informant as "brainwashing with chemicals."

However, the informant said the Gestapo wasn't satisfied with extracting information by torture. "So the next question was, why don't we do it like the Russians, who have been able to get confessions of guilt at their show trials?" They tried various barbiturates and morphine derivatives. After prisoners were fed a coffee-like substance, two of them died right away, and others died later.

The Dachau and Auschwitz experiments were written up in a lengthy report issued by the U.S. Naval Technical Mission, whose job it was at the conclusion of the war to scour all of Europe for every shred of industrial and scientific material that had been produced by the Third Reich. It was because of this report that the U.S. Navy became interested in mescaline and other drugs as a tool for interrogation. The Navy initiated Project Chatter in 1947, the same year the Central Intelligence Agency was formed. Project Chatter's program included developing methods for getting information from people against their will, but without inflicting harm or pain.

At the end of the war, the OSS was designated as the investigative unit for the International Military Tribunal, which was to become known as the Nuremberg Trials. The purpose of Nuremberg was to try the principal Nazi leaders and officers. Some Nazis were on trial for their experiments, and the U.S. was using its own "truth drugs" on these Nazi prisoners, namely Goring, Ribbentrop, Speer and eight others.

The Justice in charge of the tribunal had given the OSS permission to use the drugs. As a result, valuable information on methods to control human beings were obtained. Most of the records detailing the Nazi mind control secrets have never been publicly released. However, evidence over the following years suggests that these secret mind control methods have been used and perfected by various military, intelligence and government operations.

CHAPTER TWO

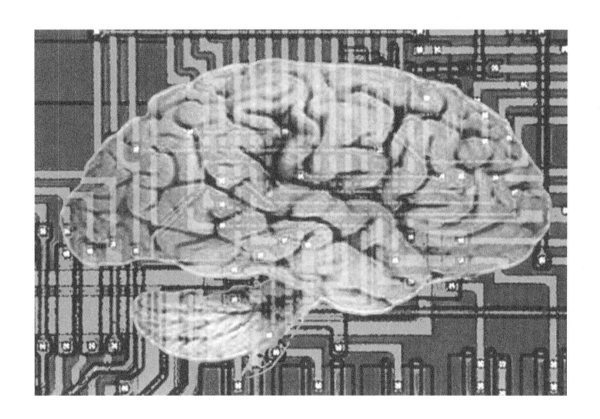

SECRET EXPERIMENTS WITH DRUGS

MIND STALKERS

We must always remember to thank the CIA and the Army for LSD. That's what people forget, they invented LSD to control people, and what they really gave us was freedom.

John Lennon

MIND STALKERS

In 1977, a Senate subcommittee on Health and Scientific Research, chaired by Senator Ted Kennedy, focused on the CIA's testing of LSD on unwitting citizens. Only a mere handful of people within the CIA knew about the scope and details of the program. The Kennedy subcommittee learned about the CIA Operation MK-ULTRA through the testimony of Dr. Sidney Gottlieb.

The purpose of the program, according to his testimony, was to "investigate whether and how it was possible to modify an individual's behavior by covert means." Claiming the protection of the National Security Act, Dr. Gottlieb was unwilling to tell the Senate subcommittee what had been learned by these experiments.

He did state, however, that the program was initially started by a concern that the Soviets and other enemies of the United States would get ahead of the U.S. in this field. Through the Freedom of Information Act, researchers were able to obtain documents detailing the MK-ULTRA program and other CIA behavior modification projects.

In 1953, CIA director Allen Dulles, speaking before a national meeting of Princeton alumni, distinguished two fronts in the then-current "battle for men's minds." A "first front" of mass indoctrination through censorship and propaganda, and a "second front" of individual "brainwashing" and "brain changing." The same year, at CIA deputy director Richard Helm's suggestion, Dulles approved the MK-ULTRA project, and exempted it from normal CIA financial controls.

BRAINWASHING

Over the years it has been understood that a powerful tool for inducing ideological and behavioral change is social pressure in a controlled environment. To establish a "cover story" for continuing this research, the CIA funded a propaganda effort designed to convince the world that the Communist Bloc had devised insidious new methods of reshaping the human will, the CIA's own efforts could therefore, if exposed, be explained as an attempt to "catch up" with the Soviets work. The primary promoter of this "line" was one Edward Hunter, a CIA contract employee operating underground as a journalist, and, later, a prominent member of the John Birch Society.

MIND STALKERS

Hunter offered "brainwashing" as the explanation for the many confessions signed by American prisoners of war during the Korean War and (generally) recanted upon the prisoners' repatriation. These confessions alleged that the United States used germ warfare in the Korean conflict, a claim which the American public of the time found impossible to accept.

Many years later investigative reporters discovered that Japan's germ warfare specialists had been brought into the American national security apparatus, and that the knowledge gleaned from Japan's horrifying germ warfare experiments probably was used in Korea, just as the "brainwashed" soldiers had said.

The conclusion is that the entire brainwashing scare of the 1950s constituted a CIA hoax perpetrated upon the American public. CIA deputy director Richard Helms admitted as much when, in 1963, he told the Warren Commission that Soviet mind control research consistently lagged years behind American efforts. Yet this simple program was enough to crank up the brainwashing scare in the United States, designed to give the CIA the political space needed to research more sophisticated mind-control techniques.

The Introduction Of LSD

The most daring phase of the MK-ULTRA program involved slipping unwitting American citizens LSD in various situations. The idea for the series of experiments had
in fact predated MK-ULTRA, originating in November 1941. At that time the OSS had invested $5000 for research for a workable "truth drug" program. Experiments with scopolamine and morphine proved both unfruitful and very dangerous. Many test subjects died after being treated with the powerful narcotics.

The program tested scores of other drugs, including mescaline, barbiturates, Benzedrine, and cannabis to name a few. The U.S. was highly concerned over the heavy losses of freighters and other ships in the North Atlantic, all victims of German U-boats. Information about German U-boat strategy was desperately needed and it was believed that the information could be obtained through drug-influenced interrogations of German naval POWS, in violation of the Geneva Accords. The Central Intelligence Agency held two major interests in use of LSD to alter normal behavior patterns. The first interest centered around obtaining information from prisoners of war and enemy agents. The second was to learn the effectiveness of drugs used against the enemy on the battlefield.

The MK-ULTRA program was originally run by a small number of people within the CIA known as the Technical Services Staff (TSS). Another CIA department, the Office of Security, also began its own testing program. Friction arose and then infighting broke out when the Office of Security commenced to spy on TSS people after it was learned that LSD was being tested on unwitting Americans. Not only did the two branches disagree over the issue of testing the drug on the unsuspecting victims, they also disagreed over the issue of how the drug was actually to be used by the CIA.

The office of Security envisioned the drug as an interrogation weapon. However, the TSS group thought the drug could be used to help destabilize another country. LSD could be slipped into the food or beverage of a public official in order to make him behave foolishly or oddly in public. One CIA document revealed that LSD could be administered right before an official was to make a public speech. The document then listed several different methods that had been secretly tested on public officials both in the United States and abroad. The tests were all considered successful.

Realizing that gaining information about the drug in real life situations was crucial to exploiting the drug to its fullest, TSS started conducting experiments on its own people. There was an extensive amount of self-experimentation. The Office of Security felt the TSS group was playing with fire, especially when it was learned that TSS was preparing to spike the CIA's annual office Christmas party punch with LSD. LSD can produce serious disorientation for periods of eight to 18 hours and possibly longer, and several people at the party became extremely ill.

One of the "victims" of the punch was agent Frank Olson. Having never had drugs before, LSD took its toll on Olson. He reported that, every car that came by was a terrible monster with fantastic eyes, out to get him personally. Each time a car passed he would huddle down against the curb, terribly frightened. Olson began to behave

MIND STALKERS

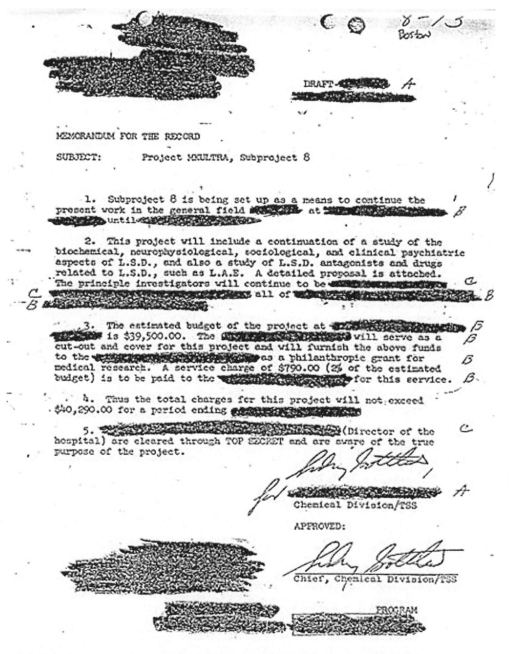

MEMORANDUM FOR THE RECORD

SUBJECT: Project MKULTRA, Subproject 8

1. Subproject 8 is being set up as a means to continue the present work in the general field [REDACTED] at [REDACTED] until [REDACTED]

2. This project will include a continuation of a study of the biochemical, neurophysiological, sociological, and clinical psychiatric aspects of L.S.D., and also a study of L.S.D. antagonists and drugs related to L.S.D., such as L.A.E. A detailed proposal is attached. The principle investigators will continue to be [REDACTED] all of [REDACTED]

3. The estimated budget of the project at [REDACTED] is $39,500.00. The [REDACTED] will serve as a cut-out and cover for this project and will furnish the above funds to the [REDACTED] as a philanthropic grant for medical research. A service charge of $790.00 (2% of the estimated budget) is to be paid to the [REDACTED] for this service.

4. Thus the total charges for this project will not exceed $40,290.00 for a period ending [REDACTED]

5. [REDACTED] (Director of the hospital) are cleared through TOP SECRET and are aware of the true purpose of the project.

Chemical Division/TSS

APPROVED:

Chief, Chemical Division/TSS

PROGRAM

Of the few surviving top-secret MKULTRA documents, many reveal an extensive interest in the drug LSD and its potential for mind control.

MIND STALKERS

strange and erratically. The CIA made preparation to treat Olson at Chestnut Lodge, but before they could, Olson checked into a New York hotel and threw himself out from his tenth story room. Afterwards, the CIA was ordered to cease all drug testing.

Even though the CIA openly halted their drug experiments, scientists working for the agency secretly continued the experiments. One researcher was Dr. Ewen Cameron, working at McGill University in Montreal. Dr. Cameron used a variety of experimental techniques, including using drugs to keep subjects unconscious for months at a time, administering huge electro shocks and continual doses of LSD.

Massive lawsuits developed as a result of this testing, and many of the subjects who suffered trauma had never agreed to participate in the experiments. Such CIA experiments infringed upon the much-honored Nuremberg Code concerning medical ethics. Ironically, Dr. Cameron was a member of the Nuremberg Tribunal. According to the Regina, Saskatchewan newspaper *The Leader Post*, five Canadians were involved with a lawsuit saying that the CIA was involved with LSD experiments in the 1950's. In the December 13, 1980 edition, *The Leader Post* reported the claims by Robert Logie, who said he was a guinea pig for the United States Central Intelligence Agency, and constantly relived the nightmare of hospital brainwashing sessions that included hallucinogenic injections and massive electric shocks.

Logie and four other Canadians launched a $5 million suit in Washington against the U.S. government. They are asking for $1 million each in damages from what they say was a CIA funded, multi-million-dollar research experiment into the behavior of drug-induced patients.

Logie, a 42-year-old reclusive bachelor, said during an interview that his troubles are connected to the Montreal hospital LSD experiments he was subjected to in the late 50s. Logie says he was a "human guinea pig" for a CIA drug experiment program called MKULTRA Sub Project 68, one of a series of CIA-sponsored schemes to test interrogation, behavior control and brainwashing. He said the CIA paid Dr. Ewen Cameron at least $60,000 to conduct the mind-control experiments and an additional $35,000 went to McGill University in the form of grants to the psychiatry department.

MIND STALKERS

Logie said a U.S. agency called the Society for the Investigation of Human Ecology was a front organization for the CIA program. Logie said he arrived here in 1968 with no knowledge of who he was or where he was. He said he "slept under a bridge for five nights before going to the police." A Vancouver relative identified him after a newspaper printed his photograph. "I don't know if my amnesia is related to the LSD experiments," he said. "All I know is that the nightmare never stops." The men's lawsuit was later thrown out of court due to lack of evidence.

LSD research was also conducted at the Addiction Research Center of the U.S. Public Health Service in Lexington, Kentucky. This institution was one of several used by the CIA. The National Institute of Mental Health and the U.S. Navy secretly funded this operation. Vast supplies of LSD and other hallucinogenic drugs were required to keep the experiment's active.

It has been reported that enough LSD was manufactured during this period to dose every citizen in the United States at least a dozen times. No one knows for sure if all the LSD was used strictly for experiments or if it was also used on so-called social troublemakers and other political dissidents.

Dr. Harris Isbell, who was a member of the Food and Drug Administration's Advisory Committee on the Abuse of Depressant and Stimulants Drugs, ran the program. Almost all of the inmates being used as test subjects were African-American. In many cases, LSD dosage was increased daily for 75 days straight.

Some fifteen hundred U.S. soldiers were also victims of drug experimentation. Some claimed they had agreed to become guinea pigs only through pressure from their superior officers. Many claimed they suffered from severe depression and other psychological stress long after the conclusion of the research program.

One such effected soldier was Master Sergeant Jim Stanley. LSD was put in Stanley's water and he "freaked out." Stanley's hallucinations continued even after he returned to his regular duties. His service record suffered, his marriage went on the rocks and he ended up beating his wife and children. It was not until 17 years later that Stanley was informed by the military that he had been used for secret LSD experiments.

MIND STALKERS

Stanley tried to sue the government, but the Supreme Court ruled no soldier could sue the Army for the LSD experiments. However, Justice William Brennen disagreed with the Court decision. He wrote, "Experimentation with unknowing human subjects is morally and legally unacceptable."

Private James Thornwell was given LSD in a military test in 1961. For the next 23 years he lived in a mental fog, eventually drowning in a Vallejo swimming pool in 1984. Large scale LSD tests on American soldiers were conducted at Aberdeen Proving Ground in Maryland, Fort Benning, Georgia, Fort Leavenworth, Kansas, Dugway Proving Ground, Utah, and in Europe and the Pacific. The Army conducted a series of LSD tests at Fort Bragg in North Carolina.

The purpose of the tests was to find out how well soldiers could perform their tasks on the battlefield while under the influence of LSD. At Fort McClellan, Alabama, 200 officers in the Chemical Corps were given LSD in order to familiarize them with the drug's effects.

At Edgewood Arsenal, soldiers were given LSD and then confined to sensory deprivation chambers and later exposed to harsh interrogation sessions by intelligence people. In these sessions, it was discovered that soldiers would cease all resistance and cooperate if promised to stop being forced to take LSD.

In Operation Derby Hat, foreign nationals accused of drug trafficking were given LSD by the Special Purpose Team, with one subject begging to be killed in order to end his ordeal. Such experiments were also conducted in Saigon on Viet Cong. POWs. One of the most potent drugs in the U.S. arsenal is called BZ or quinuclidinyl benzilate. It is a long-lasting drug and brings on a litany of psychotic experiences and almost completely isolates any person from his environment.

The main effects of BZ last up to 80 hours compared to eight hours for LSD. Negative aftereffects may persist for up to six weeks. The BZ experiments were conducted on soldiers at Edgewood Arsenal for 16 years. Many of the "victims" claim that the drug permanently affected their lives in a negative way. It so disorientated one paratrooper that he was found taking a shower in his uniform.

MIND STALKERS

BZ was eventually tested in hand grenades and 750 pound cluster bombs. Other configurations were made for mortars, artillery and missiles. The bomb was tested in Vietnam and CIA documents show it was prepared for use by the U.S. in the event of large-scale civilian uprisings. This, and other such "drug" weapons are still stockpiled, ready for use against civilians if the need should ever arise.

Another drug developed for use against civilians was the "terror drug" Anectine. In small doses, Anectine serves as a muscle relaxant. In huge doses, it produces prolonged seizure of the respiratory system and a sensation "worse than dying." The drug goes to work within 30 to 40 seconds by paralyzing the small muscles of the fingers, toes, and eyes, and then moves into the intercostal muscles and the diaphragm. The heart rate subsides to 60 beats per minute, respiratory arrest sets in and the patient remains completely conscious throughout the ordeal, which lasts two to five minutes. Those who experienced the effects of Anectine never forgot the mind-numbing terror.

Several mind-altering drugs were originally developed for non-psychoactive purposes. Some of these drugs are Phenothiazine and Thorazine. The side effects of these drugs can be a living hell to those unfortunate enough to be given large doses. The effects include the feeling of drowsiness, disorientation, shakiness, dry mouth, blurred vision and an inability to concentrate. Drugs like Prolixin are described by users as "sheer torture" and "becoming a zombie."

The Veterans Administration Hospital has been implicated by the General Accounting Office to have used heavy dosages of psychotherapeutic drugs on their patients. One patient was taking eight different drugs, three antipsychotic, two antianxiety, one antidepressant, one sedative and one anti-Parkinson. Three of these drugs were being given in dosages equal to the maximum recommended.

One report tells of a patient who refused to take the drug. "I told them I don't want the drug to start with, they grabbed me and strapped me down and gave me a forced intramuscular shot of Prolixin. They gave me Artane to counteract the Prolixin and they gave me Sinequan, which is a kind of tranquilizer to make me calm down, which over calmed me, so rather than letting up on the medication, they then gave me Ritalin to pep me up."

MIND STALKERS

Prolixin effects can last for up to two weeks. One patient describes how the drug does not calm or sedate, but instead attacks from so deep inside you, you cannot place the source of the pain. "The drugs turn your nerves in upon you. Against your will, your resistance, your resolve, all are directed at your own tissues, your own muscles, reflexes, etc."

The patient continued, "The pain grinds into your fiber, your vision is so blurred you cannot read. You ache with restlessness, so that you feel you have to walk, to pace. And then as soon as you start pacing, the opposite occurs to you, you must sit and rest. Soon, you can think of nothing else but the pain that is coursing through every cell of your body. Back and forth, up and down, you go in pain you cannot find or hope to stop. In such wretched anxiety you are overwhelmed because you cannot get relief of any kind, even in breathing."

Another drug researched for possible mind control uses was Tetrahydrocannabinol-acetate (THC), a colorless, odorless marijuana extract that was used to lace a cigarette or food substance without detection. Initially, the experiments were done on volunteer U.S. Army and OSS personnel, and testing was also disguised as a remedy for shell shock.

The experiments were so hush-hush, that only a few top officials knew about them. President Franklin Roosevelt was made aware of the experiments only after the fact. The "truth drug" however, only achieved mixed success. The experiments were halted when a memo was written: "The drug defies all but the most expert and search analysis, and for all practical purposes can be considered beyond analysis." The OSS did not halt the program. In 1943 field tests of the extract continued, despite the order to stop. One test was conducted by Captain George H. White, an OSS agent and ex-law enforcement official. His victim was August Del Grazio, a.k.a. Augie Dallas, a New York gangster. Cigarettes laced with THC were offered to Augie without his knowledge. Augie, who had served time in prison for assault and murder, had been one of the world's most notorious drug dealers and smugglers. He operated an opium factory in Turkey, and he was a leader in the underworld on the Lower East Side of New York.

MIND STALKERS

Under the influence of the drug, Augie revealed volumes of information about the underworld operations, including the names of high-ranking officials who took bribes from the mob.

These experiments encouraged the agency to continue the research. A new memo was issued: "Cigarette experiments indicated that we had a mechanism which offered promise in relaxing prisoners to be interrogated. Cigarettes offer a perfect solution in administering the correct dosage of a drug to a person with little risk of overdosing." When the OSS was disbanded after the war, Captain White continued to administer behavior modifying drugs. White's service record shows that he worked with the OSS, and by 1954 he was a high ranking Federal Narcotics Bureau officer who had been loaned to the CIA on a part-time basis.

Sex And Drugs

White rented an apartment in Greenwich Village equipped with one-way mirrors, surveillance gadgets and disguised himself as a sailor. White drugged his acquaintances with LSD and brought them back to his apartment. In 1955, the operation shifted to San Francisco. In San Francisco, "safehouses" were established under the code name Operation Midnight Climax.

Midnight Climax hired prostitute addicts who lured men from bars back to the safehouses after their drinks had been spiked with LSD. White secretly filmed the events in the safehouses. The purpose of these "national security brothels" was to enable the CIA to experiment with the act of lovemaking for extracting information from men.

In 1963, CIA Inspector General John Earman criticized Richard Helms, the father of the MK-ULTRA project. Earman charged that the new director, John McCone, had not been fully briefed on the project when he took office and that "the concepts involved in manipulating human behavior are found by many people within and outside the Agency to be distasteful and unethical." He said that "the rights and interests of U.S. citizens are placed in jeopardy."

MIND STALKERS

The Inspector General stated that LSD had been tested on individuals at all social levels, high and low, native American and foreign. Earman's criticisms were rebuffed by Helms, who warned, "Positive operation capacity to use drugs is diminishing owing to a lack of realistic testing. Tests were necessary to keep up with the Soviets."

Upon leaving government service in 1966, Captain White wrote a startling letter to his superior. In his letter to Dr. Gottlieb, Captain White reminisced about his work in the safehouses with LSD. His comments were thought provoking and disturbing.

"I was a very minor missionary, actually a heretic, but I toiled wholeheartedly in the vineyards because it was fun, fun, fun. Where else could a red-blooded American boy lie, kill, cheat, steal, rape and pillage with the sanction and blessing of the all-highest?"

The Innocents

Some of the incidents referred to by White may have been detailed on March 15, 1995, in Washington, D.C. In unpublicized sessions before the President's Committee on Radiation, New Orleans therapist Valerie Wolf introduced two of her patients who had uncovered memories of being part of extensive CIA brainwashing programs as young children (in one case, starting at age seven). Their brainwashing included torture, rape, electroshock, powerful drugs, hypnosis and death threats.

According to their testimony, the CIA then induced amnesia to prevent their recalling these terrifying sessions. Some of the researchers alleged to have conducted these experiments include:

- Dr. Robert Heath of Tulane University. As early as 1955, while working for the Army, Dr. Heath gave patients LSD while he had electrodes implanted deep inside their brains.

- Canadian researcher, Dr. Ewan Cameron. Under long-term CIA contract, attempted to depattern, and reprogram his psychiatric patients personalities. He started with 15 to 65 days of "sleep therapy," during which a patient was kept under nearly 24 hours a day, through the administration of cocktails of Thorazine, Nembutal, Seconal, Veronal, and Phenergam. Throughout this sleep period, the patient would be awakened several times a day for electroshock treatments, given at an intensity 20-40 times the normal strength.

■ Paul Hoch, M.D. A man who would become Commissioner of Mental Hygiene for the State of New York. In the 1950's, Hoch was a researcher in the field for the CIA. Dr. Hoch gave a pseudo neurotic schizophrenic patient mescaline. The patient had a familiar heaven-and-hell journey on the compound. However, Hoch followed this up with a transorbital leucotomy on the patient. Hoch also gave a patient LSD, and a local anesthetic, and then proceeded to remove pieces of cerebral cortex, asking at various moments whether the patient's perceptions were changing.

Both Wolf and her patients stated that they recovered the memories of this CIA program without regression or hypnosis techniques. Apparently these patients spontaneously discovered this information about themselves and their pasts.

Although the committee was mainly concerned with radiation, they permitted Valerie and her patients to testify because, astonishingly, several doctors who had administered the mind-control experiments had also been identified by other Americans secretly exposed to radiation.

Prominent names surfaced in the March 15 testimony: Richard Helms, former head of the CIA, Dr. Sidney Gottlieb, who ran MK-ULTRA and Dr. John Gittinger, Gottlieb's protege. These men and others were directly accused of participating in mind-control experiments on children. Predictably, this testimony received no media attention. Allegedly, MK-ULTRA was involved in the experimentation on selected American children, as well as children from Mexico and South America.

MIND STALKERS

These children were used over a period of about 40 years, starting around 1954. In fact, the program under a different name may still be continuing today. Doctors and agents who administered the program wanted to obtain control over the minds of these children, ostensibly to create super-agents who wouldn't remember secret missions they carried out. A large portion of the original research was believed to have been conducted by Nazi Germany in several death Camps. Documents detailing the experiments were no doubt found by the United States and put to use by various intelligence agencies.

Children were allegedly trained as sex agents. With the job of blackmailing prominent Americans, primarily politicians, businessmen and educators. A great deal of photography and filming was done for this purpose. Eventually, people from the inner core of the CIA program filmed each other, and some of the centers where children were used as sex agents got out of control and turned into CIA-operated sex rings. The fate of some of the children was that they were considered expendable and murdered.

One person who states that he was in this program as a child said, off the record: "They tried out their brainwashing techniques on the kids from Mexico and South America. They were considered expendable. But on another level of the program, they went after the best and the brightest American kids. Making perfect agents to combat the Soviets wasn't, I don't think, their ultimate objective. I think they were choosing the best and brightest, maybe they figured these kids would one day rise to important positions in the society, and they wanted to gain long-term control over them, so they would be under their thumb, so they could tap them at will, a way of controlling the future society."

Other people who said that they had been used as children in the program remembered that doctors with German accents were definitely present at the sessions. One therapist, who shared this information informally with colleagues around the country, states that, so far, the oldest person in the program is now 52, the youngest is now nine. Since a number of people who were brainwashed, tortured and drugged in these experiment's try to resolve their experiences in therapy, psychiatrists and other professional therapists are hearing these stories.

MIND STALKERS

They are told, for example, that CIA controllers sometimes dressed up in Satanic costumes to further traumatize the children, this also provided a cover that wouldn't be believed if the children ever talked about their experiences. In the 1970's and 80's a rash of recovered memory reports began to circulate within the mental health community. People were "remembering" childhood physical and sexual abuse by supposedly Satanic groups. However, how accurate were these reports?

How Accurate Is Recovered Memory?

Not everyone believes in the "recovered" memory's scenario. The most prominent group, the False Memory Syndrome Foundation (FMSF), have several board members with CIA or military-intelligence connections, including Dr. Louis "Jolly" West of UCLA, who tried to establish a center for "the study of violence" at the university in the 1970s. This center's specialty would have been psychosurgery, the surgical removal of brain connections, supposedly to curb people's "violent tendencies."

FMSF maintains that a person always remembers abuse done to him or her, and therefore any new recovery of it in therapy is false and must have been fabricated through misleading suggestions by the therapist. While it is certainly true that such inducement happens in therapy, the blanket statement that all recovered memory is invented is unsubstantiated. However, it has been shown that a substantial number of recovered memory cases, especially some of the more lurid stories, have been shown to be out and out hoaxes or manipulations by overzealous social workers.

In a written statement to Dr. Wolf that was included in her testimony to the President's committee, well-known researcher and psychiatrist, Colin Ross said:

"Published articles in my files include descriptions of administration of 150 mcg of LSD to children age 5-10 years on a daily basis for days, weeks, months, and in a few cases even years. Neurosurgeons at Tulane, Yale, and Harvard did extensive research on brain electrode implants with intelligence funding, and combined brain implants with large numbers of drugs including hallucinogens." Ross based his report on his more than 20 years of investigating CIA mind control.

MIND STALKERS

Chris De Nicola, one of Dr. Wolf's patients who testified before the president's committee, named her controller as a Dr. Greene, a name reported by several other mind-control subjects. It may be that this name was a cover used by various CIA and military-contracted experimenter-torturers.

"Dr. Greene used me when I was eight years old in radiation experiments both for the purpose of determining the effects of radiation on various parts of my body, and to terrorize me as an additional trauma in the mind-control experiments. The experiments took place in Tucson, Arizona, out in the desert. I was taught how to pick locks, be secretive, use my photographic memory to remember things and a technique to withhold information by repeating numbers to myself. Dr. Greene moved on to wanting me to kill dolls that looked like real children. I stabbed a doll with a spear once after being severely tortured, but the next time I refused. He used many techniques but as I got older I resisted more and more.

"He often tied me down in a cage, which was near his office. Between 1972 and 1976 he and his assistants were sometimes careless and left the cage unlocked. Whenever physically possible, I snuck into his office and found files with reports and memos addressed to CIA and military personnel. Included in these files were project, subject and experiment names with some code numbers for radiation mind-control experiments which I have submitted in my written documentation.

"I was caught twice and Dr. Greene tortured me ruthlessly with electric shock, drugs, spinning on a table, putting shots in my stomach, in my back, dislocating my joints and hypnotic techniques to make me feel crazy and suicidal."

Claudia Mullin, the other of Dr. Wolf's patients who testified before the President's Committee on Radiation, said her experiences with CIA mind-control experiences began when she was seven years old.

"In 1958, I was to be tested, they told me by some important doctors coming from a place called the 'Society' (the Human Ecology Society, a CIA front). I was told to cooperate, and answer any of their questions. Then, since the test 'might hurt,' I would be given shots, x-rays, and a few jolts of electricity.

MIND STALKERS

"I was instructed not to look at anyone's face too hard and to ignore names, as this was a very secret project and I had to be brave and all those things would help me forget. Dr. John Gittinger tested me and a Dr. Cameron gave me the shocks and Dr. Greene the x-rays. By the time I left to go home, just like every time from then on, I would recall nothing of my tests or the different doctors. I would only remember whatever explanations Dr. Robert G. Heath (of Tulane Medical School) gave me for the odd bruises, needle marks, burns on my head and fingers and even the genital soreness. I had no reason to believe otherwise. Already they had begun to control my mind.

"The next year, I was sent to a place in Maryland called Deep Creek Cabins to learn how to 'sexually please men.'' Also, I was taught how to coerce them into talking about themselves. It was Richard Helms (Deputy Director of the CIA), Dr. Gottlieb, Captain George White and Morse Allen, who all planned on filming as many high government and agency officials and heads of academic institutions and foundations as possible. I was to become a regular little 'spy' for them, after that summer, eventually entrapping many unwitting men, including themselves, all with the use of a hidden camera. I was only nine when this kind of sexual humiliation began."

Ms. Mullin states that she was adopted when she was two years old. By the time she reached seven she had already been abused extensively by her mother. Her mother apparently turned her over for "testing" to CIA-connected people and Claudia then entered a 27-year period of what can only be called enslavement. Claudia states that she has been monitored, that she is still monitored and watched by agency related people, including a medical doctor. Now living in New Orleans, she has given information to local police authorities about her situation. In her testimony to the President's committee, Claudia remarked, "Although the process of recalling these atrocities is certainly not an easy task, nor is it without some danger to myself and my family, I feel the risk is worth taking. It will be more difficult to conduct such programs in the future because of what we do now."

Claudia's therapist, Dr. Wolf, has written to the President's committee, "To the best of my knowledge, Claudia has read nothing about mind-control or CIA covert

operations. Since she decided to listen carefully and remember as much as she could about conversations among the researchers, her memories are extraordinarily complete. I have sent written copies of memories to Dr. Alan Scheflin (author of *The Mind Manipulators*) for validation and he has confirmed that she has knowledge of events and people that are not published anywhere, that some of her memories contain new
information and that some are already known and published. Some of her memories have been confirmed by family members. She has also shown me old scrapbooks where she wrote notes to remember what was happening to her and hid the notes under pictures in the scrapbook."

Dr. Wolf also noted that when word got around she was going to testify before the President's committee, she was contacted by about 40 therapists "in just the 10 days leading up to my trip to Washington." The therapists had heard similar CIA mind-control stories from their own patients. Many of these professionals are afraid to go on the record about their patients' stories, as censure from their professional societies is a reality. The political mood these days is not conducive to granting any kind of credibility to revelations of CIA brainwashing.

CHAPTER THREE

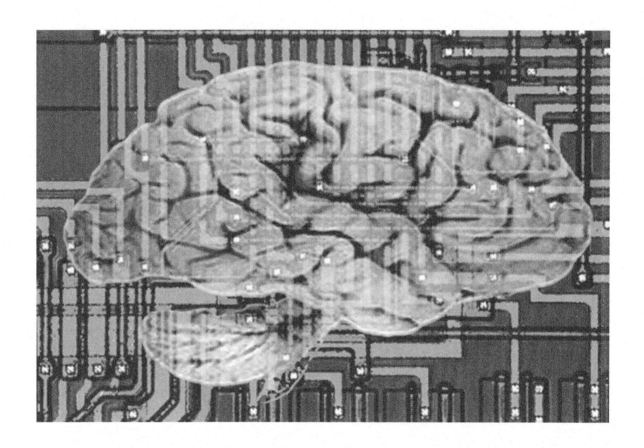

SUBLIMINAL SEDUCTION

MIND STALKERS

I feel very strongly that we mustn't be caught by surprise by our own advance in technology. This has happened gain and again in history with technology's advance, and this changes social conditions and suddenly people have found themselves in a situation which they didn't foresee and doing all sorts of things they didn't really want to do.

Aldous Huxley

MIND STALKERS

Besides hypnosis, subliminal persuasion is best known for its reputation as a possible mind control technique. In a series of articles, Jon Elliston, editor for **Dossier**, researched the development of subliminal advertisements and the controversy that surrounded it. In 1958, the American public faced a frightening question: could subliminal messages be used to influence the unsuspecting public? Evidence seemed to confirm the power of undetected commands slipped "beneath the threshold of awareness."

It began in late 1957, when a New Jersey marketing specialist named James Vicary introduced the idea of subliminal messages to a still naive public. Vicary had conducted market research on groups of shoppers, and attracted some attention for his studies of the eye-blink rate of female customers in various store settings. Those tests seemed to show that people could unconsciously perceive quick flashes of information.

In 1957, Vicary announced that he had designed a subliminal projection machine, capable of flashing unnoticeable messages within big-screen movies.   When he tried out his new method he claimed to have increased concession sales by flashing one or two frame messages like "Eat Popcorn" and "Drink Coke" during the films. Vicary later downplayed the effectiveness of the technique and admitted that his research data on subliminal projection was "too small to be meaningful." Subliminal mania spread like a wildfire across the national consciousness, as people began to wonder "What do I see that I don't notice, and what can it do to me?"

Official Reaction

The broadcasting industry quickly recognized the fact that whatever profit they might make with subliminal advertising would be soon canceled out by the developing stigma associated with the technique. In November 1957 the National Association of Radio and Television Broadcasters asked its 300 member stations to refrain from using subliminal advertising pending "review and consideration" by the group.

The memo requesting the ban cautioned that subliminal messages could frighten consumers and hurt advertiser's credibility: "A very serious problem is the reaction of the public to having subliminal advertising thrust upon them. There may be grave concern over the idea of advertising which affects people below their level of conscious awareness, so that they are not able to exercise conscious control over their acceptance or rejection of the messages."

It wasn't long before politicians in Washington, D.C. decided to get involved. Legislators led by Utah Representative William Dawson started a drive to ban subliminal broadcasting, which he called the "secret pitch." Dawson spoke of the "frightening aspects" of subliminal messages. "Put to political propaganda purposes," he warned, "subliminal communication would be made to order for the establishment and maintenance of a totalitarian government."

No one knew at the time if subliminal messages had the potential for mind control, so the attitude among lawmakers was: "since we know so little about the process, we had better restrict its use now and let researchers find out what it can really do later on." This attitude has surfaced time and again with Congress and other politicians who rarely stay ahead on scientific progress and thus are more prone to passing laws based on ignorance. In an attempt to allay Congress's fears and save his invention, James Vicary took his subliminal show to the nation's capital where several members of Congress and FCC chairman John Doerfer viewed a demonstration of the technique. In a Washington television studio, Vicary showed the group a few minutes of a movie with split-second "Eat Popcorn" messages inserted in the film. During the screening, Senator Charles E. Potter of Michigan quipped: "I think I want a hot dog." Jokes aside, Potter said he believed the technique should not be used on television until federal regulations were established.

Vicary took the occasion to downplay the power of subliminal advertisements, calling them "a mild form of advertising" and "a very weak persuader." The man behind the outbreak of subliminal fears assured his official audience that he would insist that television viewers be informed in advance by stations who were planning to use subliminal advertisements. Vicary continued by stating that whatever power subliminal advertisements do have on people could be put to better use by spreading public service messages like "Fight Polio," or "Join the Army."

MIND STALKERS

The CIA'S Assessment

Even though the development of subliminal persuasion has been credited to James Vicary, there is sufficient evidence that suggests the intelligence community was already very familiar with the technique through years of previous research. The CIA's internal publication on the history and methodology of the intelligence business called: *Studies in Intelligence*, carried a report in the Spring 1958 issue by CIA officer Richard Gafford entitled: *The Operational Potential of Subliminal Perception*.

Gafford's report for *Studies in Intelligence* was openly skeptical on the subject of subliminal influence. The report directly criticizes Vicary's claims of subliminal success: "It is evident that there are several mighty leaps in logic in the advertising man's argument, and a great many places where his scheme can go astray. He has taken several psychological phenomena which have been demonstrated to a limited degree in controlled laboratory experiments and strung them together into an appealing argument for a 'technique.'"

Gafford did not reject the feasibility of subliminal communication altogether. By 1958 the CIA had already conducted a number of secret projects researching mind control, and was familiar with how the human mind could be manipulated. "Interest in the operational potential of subliminal perception has precedent in serious consideration of the techniques of hypnosis, extrasensory perception, and various forms of conditioning," the report notes. "By each of these techniques, it has been demonstrated, certain individuals can at certain times and under certain circumstances be influenced to act abnormally without awareness of the influence or at least without antagonism."

Ultimately these methods, "although they occasionally produced dramatic results," proved unreliable, the report says. The subliminal method had its problems as well. It was difficult to select and test the right variables and to pin down the effect of secret stimuli, and apparently impossible to standardize a technique that would work with most people. The report concludes: "There are so many elusive variables and so many sources of irregularity in the device of directing subliminal messages to a target individual that its operational feasibility is exceedingly limited."

MIND STALKERS

Sex Sells

The second wave of controversy over subliminal messages hit the United States in 1973, when Wilson Bryan Key's popular book *Subliminal Seduction* resurrected subliminal hysteria. The book charged that the use of hidden messages and images in print ads is widespread and causes millions of consumers to buy products through deception.

The subliminal mechanism that concerned Key most was the "embed," a word, slogan, or symbol inserted faintly into advertisements. "You cannot pick up a newspaper, magazine, or pamphlet, hear radio, or view television without being assaulted subliminally by embeds," Key claimed.

"Subliminal messages infiltrate our minds so often," Key argued, that "as a culture, North America might well be described as one enormous, magnificent, self-service, subliminal massage parlor."

One aspect of Key's subliminal theory is the focus advertisers have in using the public's interest in sex as a subliminal hook. In a chapter titled "Sex is Alive and Embedded in Practically Everything," Key says that "SEX is the most frequently embedded word in the American advertising industry." He claims the one-word cue for lust is hidden in everything from liquor ads to Ritz crackers, the holes of which he says are arranged during baking to form several depictions of the letter's S, E, and X.

In his 1980 book *The Clam-Plate Orgy*, Key revealed more alleged subliminal sex messages. The book's title refers to a pile of deep-fried clams pictured on a Howard Johnson's place-mat. Instead of a plate of seafood, Key saw blatant suggestions of group sex and bestiality, people and animals engaged in sexual activity. In addition, Key argued, the ad copy with the picture was sexually suggestive: "A batch of succulent tender clams, piled high with creamy cole slaw and french fries." Keys' analysis may not be persuasive, but it does show some interesting ideas concerning the entire subliminal issue. Perhaps the main lesson to be learned from *Subliminal Seduction* and Key's other books is that if you look hard enough, you can see some suspicious things in all sorts of unlikely places.

CHAPTER FOUR

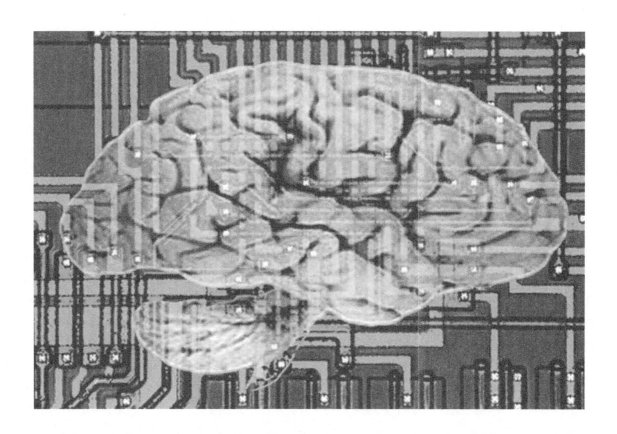

THE REAL MANCHURIAN CANDIDATE

MIND STALKERS

The day has come when we can combine sensory deprivation with the use of drugs, hypnosis, and the astute manipulation of reward and punishment to gain almost absolute control over an individual's behavior. We want to reshape our society drastically.

Dr. James V. McConnel
Director of Mental Health Research
at the University of Michigan

MIND STALKERS

Regression therapy such as that practiced by Dr. Valerie Wolf, could be considered a threat to the techniques the CIA may have secretly developed involving the use of hypnosis and mind control. Shortly after Pearl Harbor, George Estabrooks, chairman of the Department of Psychology at Colgate University, was called to Washington by the War Department. As one of the leading authorities on hypnosis, Estabrooks was asked to evaluate how it might be used by the enemy.

In 1943 he wrote a book, expanded in a second edition fourteen years later, that included a discussion of the use of hypnotism in warfare. In his opinion, one in five adult humans is capable of being placed in a trance so deep that they will have no memory of it. They could be hypnotized secretly by using a disguised technique, and given a post-hypnotic suggestion. Estabrooks suggested that a dual personality could be constructed with hypnosis, thereby creating the perfect double agent with an unshakable cover.

The Truth Uncovered

In the April 1971 issue of **Science Digest**, Estabrooks detailed how he "programmed" American spies with hypnosis. "One of the most fascinating but dangerous applications of hypnosis is its use in military intelligence. This is a field with which I am familiar through formulating guide lines for the techniques used by the United States in two world wars.

"Communication in war is always a headache. Codes can be broken. A professional spy may or may not stay bought. Your own man may have unquestionable loyalty, but his judgment is always open to question. The 'hypnotic courier,' on the other hand, provides a unique solution. I was involved in preparing many subjects for this work during World War II. One successful case involved an Army Service Corps Captain whom we'll call George Smith.

"Captain Smith had undergone months of training. He was an excellent subject but did not realize it. I had removed from him, by post-hypnotic suggestion, all recollection of ever having been hypnotized. First I had the Service Corps call the captain to Washington and tell him they needed a report of the mechanical equipment of Division X headquartered in Tokyo. Smith was ordered to leave by jet next morning, pick up the report and return at once. Consciously, that was all he knew, and it was the story he gave to his wife and friends. Then I put him under deep hypnosis, and gave him, orally, a vital message to be delivered directly on his arrival in Japan to a certain colonel, let's say his name was Brown, of military intelligence.

"Outside of myself, Colonel Brown was the only person who could hypnotize Captain Smith. This is 'locking.' I performed it by saying to the hypnotized Captain: 'Until further orders from me, only Colonel Brown and I can hypnotize you. We will use a signal phrase 'the moon is clear.' Whenever you hear this phrase from Brown or myself, you will pass instantly into deep hypnosis.' When Captain Smith reawakened, he had no conscious memory of what happened in the trance. All that he was aware of was that he must head for Tokyo to pick up a division report.

"On arrival there, Smith reported to Brown, who hypnotized him with the signal phrase. Under hypnosis, Smith delivered my message and received one to bring back. Awakened, he was given the division report and returned home by jet. There, I hypnotized him once more with the signal phrase, and he rattled off Brown's answer that had been dutifully tucked away in his unconscious mind.

"The system is virtually foolproof. As characterized by this case, the information was 'locked' in Smith's unconscious for retrieval by the only two people who knew the combination. The subject had no conscious memory of what happened, so he could not spill the beans. No one else could hypnotize him even if they might know the signal phrase. Smith was an excellent subject for the program. His situation, however, was not that unique. Probably six out of ten people would respond in the same fashion as Smith if they were placed under hypnosis and given similar commands.

"Not all applications of hypnotism to military intelligence are as tidy. Perhaps you have read *The Three Faces of Eve*. The book was based on a case reported in 1905 by Dr. Morton Prince of Massachusetts General Hospital and Harvard. He startled everyone in the field by announcing that he had cured a woman named Beauchamp of a split personality. Using post-hypnotic suggestion to submerge an incom -

patible childlike part of the patient, he'd been able to make two other sides of Mrs. Beauchamp compatible, and lump them together in a single cohesive personality.

"Clinical hypnotists throughout the world jumped on the multiple personality bandwagon as a fascinating frontier. By the 1920's, not only had they learned to apply post-hypnotic suggestion to deal with this weird problem, but also had learned how to split certain complex individuals into multiple personalities. The potential for military intelligence has been nightmarish.

"During World War II, I worked this technique with a vulnerable Marine lieutenant I'll call Jones. Under the watchful eye of Marine Intelligence, I spilt his personality into Jones A and Jones B. Jones A, once a 'normal' working Marine, became entirely different. He talked communist doctrine and meant it. He was welcomed enthusiastically by communist cells, was deliberately given a dishonorable discharge by the Corps (which was in on the plot) and became a card - carrying party member.

"The joker was Jones B, the second personality, formerly apparent in the conscious Marine. Under hypnosis, this Jones had been carefully coached by suggestion. Jones B was the deeper personality, knew all the thoughts of Jones A, was a loyal American, and was 'imprinted' to say nothing during conscious phases. All I had to do was hypnotize the whole man, get in touch with Jones B, the loyal American, and I had a pipeline straight into the Communist camp. It worked beautifully for months with this subject, but the technique backfired.

While there was no way for an enemy to expose Jones dual personality, they suspected it and played the same trick on us later. By this time the method for using dual personalities was being used by other countries as several agents from the 'other side' had already been caught.

"The use of 'waking hypnosis' in counter intelligence during World War II occasionally became so involved that it taxed even my credulity. Among the most complicated ploys used was the practice of sending a perfectly normal, wide awake agent into enemy camp, after he'd been carefully coached in waking hypnosis to act the part of a potential hypnotism subject. Trained in autosuggestion, or self-hypnosis, such a subject can pass every test used to spot a hypnotized person. Using it, he can control the rate of his heartbeat, anesthetize himself to a degree against pain of electric shock or torture.

"In the case of an officer we'll call Cox, this carefully prepared counterspy was given a title to indicate he had access to top priority information. He was planted in an international café in a border country where it was certain there would be enemy agents. He talked too much, drank a lot, made friends with local girls, and pretended a childish interest in hypnotism. The hope was that he would blunder into a situation where enemy agents would kidnap him and try to hypnotize him, in order to extract information from him.

"Cox worked so well that they fell for the trick. He never allowed himself to be hypnotized during seances. While pretending to be a hypnotized subject of the foe, he was gathering and feeding back information. Eventually, Cox did get caught, when he was followed to an information drop. And this international group plays rough. The enemy offered him a "ride" at gunpoint. There were four men in the vehicle. Cox watched for a chance, and found it when the car skirted a ravine. He leaped for the wheel, twisted it, and over the edge they went. Two of his guards were killed in the crash. In the ensuing scramble, he got hold of another man's gun, liquidated the remaining two, then hobbled across the border with nothing worse than a broken leg."

This amazing admission by George Estabrooks on the use of hypnosis to create the perfect spy or soldier, indicates that the human mind can be easily harnessed for the purpose of others. It would be hard to believe that techniques for hypnotic mind control have not been perfected in the years since those early experiments.

The Killer Within

At the time, Estabrooks was not the only one considering the potential of hypnotism on the human mind. Writing in *The Psychoanalytic Review* of 1947, Major Harvey Leavitt of the U.S. Army Medical Corps described the hypnotic creation of a secondary personality, "hypnotically induced automatic writing was established early in the course of treatment as a means of expeditiously gaining access to unconscious material. After this procedure was used for a while, a hypnotic secondary personality was produced by suggesting that the writing was under control of a certain part of his personality unaware to him." Leavitt then said that he created another personality in direct contrast to the one already established so he could work the two created personalities against one another.

He concluded, "regardless of whether the production of multiple personalities by means of hypnosis could be construed as additional proof that hypnosis is an artificially induced hysteria or whether the multiple personalities were artificial entities resulting from direct suggestions, there exists a close relationship with personalities spontaneously arising in hysterical dissociation.

The importance of producing multiple personalities experimentally lies in the fact that certain elements of the original personality may be isolated which manifest a minimum of censorship influences and thus may serve as helpful adjuncts in hypnoanalysis."

That was not the purpose for the intelligence agencies in working with the idea of creating a multiple personality. The story of the intelligence agencies creating multiple personalities to use as couriers and assassins may have begun with Estabrooks, and indeed in CIA documents you can see Estabrooks' theories worked out and discussed.

The genesis of the work begins in 1951 in the CIA Office of Security where an official named Morse Allen got the idea that CIA agents should be trained in hypnosis, and in order to do so he arranged with them to go up to New York and get training from a stage hypnotist. As soon as he and the agents got to New York, the stage hypnotist spent an hour and a half with them, regaling them with tales of hypnotic seduction.

He told them how when he went on the road, he would sleep with a different woman each night. He would give some women hypnotic suggestions that he was their husband, this was a technique he had found very productive for his own sexual favors. The CIA was delighted to hear all of this and reported so in the documents.

if the hypnotist could use the technique to manipulate people, this was what they wanted to learn. Because of this, Operation ARTICHOKE was created.

In over 2,000 pages of documentation going from 1951 to 1954, Morse Allen and his group experimented with a wide range of hypnotic processes. This ranged from using hypnosis to convince subjects to place their hands in acid or jars of snakes.

Some victims were hypnotically persuaded to commit acts of robbery and murder. The ultimate goal of the CIA was to explore the possibility of using hypnosis to create a programmed courier and a programmed assassin.

The use of hypnosis to create multiple personalities for intelligence purposes appears in a number of confidential secret documents. The CIA debunked the old theory of a hypnotic moral curb. They came to the conclusion that people can be induced to do things that would violate their moral codes, and the belief that you can't get people to do things against their will was simply untrue. Because of this, the CIA was able to carry out further experiments to ultimately create involuntary killers. These "hidden assassin" programs continue today for use in eliminating political enemies worldwide.

By 1953, Morse Allen was pushing hard to have operational tests to show that you could construct a multiple personality and have that personality commit crimes, come back, and have no knowledge of the situation. In other words, The Manchurian Candidate scenario had been worked out by the CIA five years before the novel was published.

In order to discover whether or not the Manchurian Candidate scenario could work, Allen conducted what he called "terminal experiments." These were experiments that could result in the death of the subject. The CIA willingly gave clearance for the secret experiments to be conducted. By January 1954, an ARTICHOKE memo says, "Could an individual of a certain descent be made to perform an act of attempted assassination involuntarily under the influence of ARTICHOKE?" The same memo also states, "an individual of a certain descent, approximately 35 years old, well educated, proficient in English, and well established socially and politically in a foreign government could be induced under ARTICHOKE to perform an act involuntarily of attempted assassination against a prominent foreign politician or if necessary, against an American official."

The evidence is convincing that by the summer of 1954, the ARTICHOKE team could create an artificial personality, and program that personality to conduct an assassination. If in fact the individual was captured, he would never reveal the knowledge that he had engaged in the assassination. The host would know nothing about the artificial personality, the amnesia would be impenetrable. Even under torture, the host would not, could not, reveal the secrets.

CIA research in universities around the United States, explored topics such as the possibility that preprogrammed people could be set off by way of telephone. It was shown that a person could answer a telephone, a secret word would be given, they would then slip automatically into a trance. Nobody around them would know they were in a trance. The victim wouldn't know they were in a trance. Experiments were also conducted on whether people would commit suicide under hypnotic instructions.

In May 1955, a top secret report called *Hypnotism and Covert Operations* begins with the following paragraph: "Frankly I now mistrust much of what was written by academic experts on hypnotism, partly because many of them seem to have generalized from a very few cases, and partly because much of their cautious pessimism is contradicted by Agency experimenters. But more particularly because I have personally witnessed behavior responses which experts have said are impossible to obtain."

Killers On Command

A U.S. Navy psychologist revealed in 1973 that the Office of Naval Intelligence had been taking convicted murderers from military prisons, used behavior modification techniques on them, and then relocated them in American embassies throughout the world. The Navy psychologist was Lt. Commander Thomas Narut of the U.S. Regional Medical Center in Naples, Italy. The information was released at an Oslo NATO conference of 120 psychologists from the eleven nation alliance.

MIND STALKERS

According to Dr. Narut, the U.S. Navy was an excellent place for a researcher to find "captive personnel" whom they could use as guinea pigs in experiments. "The Navy provided all the funding necessary."

Dr. Narut, in a question and answer session with reporters from around the world, revealed how the Navy was secretly programming large numbers of assassins. He said that the men he had worked with for the Navy was being prepared for commando-type operations, as well as covert operations in U.S. embassies worldwide. He described the men who went through his program as "hit men and assassins" who could kill on command.

Careful screening of the subjects was accomplished by Navy psychologists through military records. Those who actually received assignments where their training could be used, were drawn from submarine crews, the paratroops, and many were convicted murderers serving military prison sentences. Several men who had been awarded medals for bravery in the line of duty were drafted into the program.

The assassins were conditioned through "audio-visual desensitization." The process involved the showing of films of people being injured or killed in a variety of ways, starting with very mild depictions, leading up to the more extreme forms of violence. Eventually, the subjects would be able to detach their feelings even when viewing the most horrible of films.

The conditioning was most successful when applied to "passive-aggressive" types, and most of these ended up being able to kill without any regrets. The prime indicator of violent tendencies in their candidates was the Minnesota Multiphasic Personality Inventory. Dr. Narut knew of two Navy programming centers, the Neuropsychiatric laboratory in San Diego and the U.S. Regional Medical Center in Italy, where he worked.

During the audio-visual desensitization programming, which sounds reminiscent of the movie *A Clockwork Orange*, restraints were used to force the subject to view the films. A device was used on the subjects eyelids to prevent him from blinking.

MIND STALKERS

The first film involved an African youth being ritualistically circumcised with a dull knife. The film was reportedly extremely gruesome and very painful to watch. The second film showed a sawmill scene in which a man accidentally cut off his fingers. Again, the effects were realistically portrayed with graphic use of blood and gore.

In addition to the desensitization films, the potential assassins underwent programming to create prejudicial attitude in the men, to think of their future enemies, especially the leaders of these countries, as subhuman. Films and lectures were presented demeaning the culture and habits of the people of the countries where it had been decided they would be sent. This way a person can be programmed to consider the enemy as "less than human," thus eliminating any moral constraints that may exist in the assassin.

After his NATO lecture, Dr. Narut disappeared. Within a week or so after the lecture, the Pentagon issued an emphatic denial that the U.S. Navy had "engaged in psychological training or other types of training of personnel as assassins." They disavowed the programming centers in San Diego and Naples and stated they were unable to find Narut, but did provide confirmation that he was a staff member of the U.S. Regional Medical Center in Naples.

Dr. Alfred Zitani, an American delegate to the Oslo conference, did verify Narut's remarks and they were published in the Sunday Times. Sometime later, Dr. Narut surfaced again in London and recanted his remarks, stating that he was "talking in theoretical and not practical terms." Shortly afterwards, the U.S. Naval headquarters in London issued a statement saying that Dr. Narut's remarks at the NATO conference should be discounted because he had "personal problems." Dr. Narut never made any further public statements about the program.

During the NATO conference in Oslo, Dr. Narut had remarked that the reason he was divulging the information was because he believed that the information was coming out anyway. The doctor was referring to the disclosures by a Congressional subcommittee concerning various CIA assassination plots. However, what Dr. Narut had failed to realize at the time, was that the Navy's assassination plots were not destined to be revealed to the public at that time.

MIND STALKERS

Luis Castillo: Hypnotic Assassin?

Another interesting case centered on an assassin named Luis Castillo, who after his capture in the Philippines, was extensively debriefed and studied by experts in the employment of the National Bureau of Investigation, the Philippines equivalent to the FBI. Castillo was discovered to have had at least four separate personalities hypnotically instilled, each personality could be triggered by a specific cue. One personality claimed to be Sgt. Manuel Angel Ramirez, of the Strategic Air Tactical Command in South Vietnam. Supposedly, "Ramirez" was the illegitimate son of a certain pipe-smoking, highly-placed CIA official whose initials were A.D. Another personality claimed to be one of John F. Kennedy's assassins.

The main hypnotist involved with this case labeled these hypnotic alter-egos "Zombie states." The report on the case stated that "The Zombie phenomenon referred to here is a somnambulistic behavior displayed by the subject in a conditioned response to a series of words, phrases, and statements, apparently unknown to the subject during his normal waking state."

When Castillo was repatriated to the United States, the FBI claimed that he had fabricated the entire story. In his book *Operation Mind Control*, Walter Bowart makes a convincing case against the FBI's claims. Certainly, many aspects of the Castillo affair argue for his sincerity, including his hypnotically-induced insensitivity to pain. Castillo continued to insist that his story was true, and unfortunately attempted suicide several times, apparently because of buried post- hypnotic suggestions.

The Strange Case Of Candy Jones

Perhaps the most fascinating case of multiple-personality mind control, was the case of former model, Candy Jones. Ms. Jones (born Jessica Wilcox) achieved star status as a model during World War II, and later established her own modeling agency. In 1960, an FBI man requested her to allow her place of business to be used as a "mail drop" for the Bureau and "another government agency" (presumably, the CIA). Candy, supposedly deeply patriotic, accepted the arrangement.

MIND STALKERS

Her involvement on the fringes of the clandestine world eventually brought Candy into contact with a "Dr. Gilbert Jensen," who worked, in turn, with a "Dr. Marshall Burger" (Both names are pseudonyms). Unknown to her, these doctors had been employed as mind control experts by the CIA. Using a job interview as a cover, Jensen induced hypnosis, and found Candy to be a particularly responsive subject. Jensen then allegedly went on to use her as a test subject for the CIA's mind control program.

Using hypnotic techniques, Candy's personality was split into two separate entities. Candy's job was to provide a clandestine courier service for several intelligence operations. Estabrooks had outlined the basic idea years earlier:

"Induce hypnosis via a disguised technique, give the messenger information to memorize, hypnotically erase the message from conscious memory, and install a post-hypnotic suggestion that the message (now buried within the subconscious) will be brought forth only upon a specific cue. If the hypnotist can find and create such a courier, ultra-security can be guaranteed, even torture won't cause the messenger to tell what they know, because their conscious mind has no memory of the secret information."

Candy was one such success story. Success, in this context, means that she could be, and was, brutally tortured and abused while running assignments for the CIA. All that had been learned from ARTICHOKE and MK-ULTRA was brought into play, hypnosis, drugs, conditioning, and electronics. Using these devices, Jensen and Burger managed to install a duplicate personality in Jones, and create amnesia of the programming sessions and the field assignments. The hidden personality could be triggered by a telephone call with particular sounds, and after the mission was completed, the normal personality remembered nothing.

These missions were elaborate, and frequently involved world travel to deliver messages. Jones and other victims were once even subjected to torture at a seminar at CIA headquarters, as a means of demonstrating the psychiatrist's control over his subjects. The hypnotists turned Candy into a vicious, hateful bigot. This was done in order to isolate her from her friends and family. This change in Candy's personality mystified her associates, as they considered her noteworthy for her racial tolerance.

In fact, Candy's modeling agency was one of the first to break the color barrier. Friends later remembered that during this time Candy started becoming cold and distant and would disappear with no explanation for days at a time.

Jensen and Burger also managed to program Candy to commit suicide at the end of her usefulness to the Agency, in a fashion similar to the Luis Castillo case. The Human mind however, can still elude complete control. Candy's programming techniques were apparently flawed. She breached security in 1972 when she married famed New York radio personality Long John Nebel.

Nebel, suspecting something was wrong with his new wife, sought help from a friend trained in hypnotic regression techniques. After a number of sessions, the hypnotist extracted the long-repressed truth. Eventually, the "other Candy" was eliminated, and the programming broken.

Even though evidence has been uncovered that seems to validate Candy's claim of mind control, no one really knows for sure if her story was true or possibly a "false memory" brought about by the inexperience of an overeager hypnotist.

Candy Jones Secret CIA Files

Skeptics might find Candy's story incredible and unlikely. An amateur had conducted her hypnotic regression, and the possibility of "false memory" always lurks. However, the veracity of her narrative has been established beyond reasonable doubt. In her hypnotic regression sessions, she recalled being programmed at a government-connected institute in northern California. This establishment, as investigators later proved, was indeed heavily involved with government-funded brainwashing research.

Other aspects of Candy's story, especially the details of the programming methods used on her, were substantiated by documents released after the 1976 book by Donald Bain titled *The Control of Candy Jones*. Interviews with Milton Kline, Dr. Frances Jakes, John Watkins and others provided the testimony that the programming of Candy Jones was feasible. Recently, the case has received important confirmation.

MIND STALKERS

Investigators interested in follow-up research have filed FOIA requests with the CIA for all papers relating to Candy Jones. The agency admits that it has a substantial file on her, but refuses to release any part of it. If her tale is false, then why would the CIA be so reluctant to deliver the information? Why would they have a file on Candy Jones in the first place? Other cases with similarities to the Candy Jones story have been reported. The disturbing question is how many other innocent victims of hypnotic manipulation are unknowingly being used to further someone else's secret agenda?

The final confirmation of Candy's tale was the revelation after his death that "Marshall Burger" was really Dr. William Kroger. Kroger, long associated with the espionage establishment, had written the following in 1963, "a good subject can be hypnotized to deliver secret information. The memory of this message could be covered by an artificially induced amnesia. In the event that he should be captured, he naturally could not remember that he had ever been given the message. However, since he had been given a post-hypnotic suggestion, the message would be subject to recall through a specific cue." If Candy made up her story, why did she name this scientist, who, writing theoretically in 1963, predicted the subsequent events in her life?

After the Candy Jones affair, Kroger transferred his base of operations to UCLA, specifically to the Neuropsychiatric Institute run by Dr. Louis Jolyon West, an MK-ULTRA veteran. There he wrote *Hypnosis and Behavior Modification*, with a preface by Martin Orne and H.J. Eysenck (both MK-ULTRA veterans). The final chapter of Kroger's book contains chilling hints of the possibilities inherent in combining hypnosis with electronics, implants, and conditioning, though Kroger is careful to point out that "we are not concerned that man might be conditioned by rewards and punishments through electronic brain stimulation to be controlled like robots." A frightening prediction of things to come. The power to secretly influence the human mind invites abuse. What individual or group seeking power, or wishing to maintain power, could resist the ability to secretly control others? If reports of hidden assassins are true, then all cases of "lone nut" assassinations over the last fifty years should be reinvestigated. The assassinations of John Kennedy, Robert Kennedy, Martin Luther King and the attempted killings of Presidents Ford and Reagan could all be considered "murders by mind control."

Using hypnotic techniques, Candy Jone's personality was split into two separate entities. Candy's job was to provide a clandestine courier service for several intelligence operations.

CHAPTER FIVE

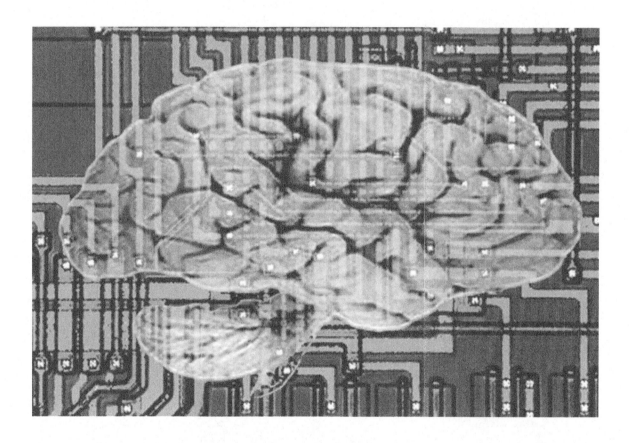

ELECTRONICS, MICROWAVES, AND IMPLANTS

MIND STALKERS

Man does not have the right to develop his own mind. This kind of liberal orientation has great appeal. We must electrically control the brain. Some day armies and generals will be controlled by electric stimulation of the brain.

Dr. Jose Delgado
February 24, 1974 edition
The Congressional Record
No. 26., Vol. 118

MIND STALKERS

On December 17, 1997 in Japan, more than 700 people, mainly school children, were rushed to hospitals after suffering convulsions, vomiting, irritated eyes and other symptoms after watching **Pokemon**, a popular cartoon based on Nintendo's "Pocket Monsters" video game. Two-hundred people, from age three to a 58-year-old man, remained in the hospital for several days with epilepsy-type symptoms more than 24 hours after the showing, the Home Affairs Ministry said. **Pokemon** is Japan's most highly-rated program in its 6:30 PM time slot.

The December 17 episode, *Computer Warrior Porigon*, featured characters fighting inside a computer. Most of the children developed the symptoms about 20 minutes into the program after a scene depicting an exploding "vaccine bomb" set off to destroy a computer virus. It was followed by five seconds of flashing red light in the eyes of "Pikachu," a rat-like creature that is the show's most popular character. Some other children were stricken later, when watching excerpts from the scene in TV news reports on the earlier victims.

TV Tokyo programming division manager Hironari Mori said the offending section passed inspection before broadcast, but in hindsight "we believe there may have been problems with presentation and production technique." Mori also said, "I must say that as an adult that part made me blink, so for a child the effect must have been considerable."

Dr. Yukio Fukuyama, a juvenile epilepsy expert, said that "television epilepsy" can be triggered by flashing, colorful lights. Though the phenomenon was observed before television, photosensitive epilepsy, as it is also called, has become far more common as TV has spread. The same symptoms have also been observed in children playing video games. During the 1980's several cases of "video-game induced epilepsy" were reported in the media and medical journals. Fukuyama says parents should be made aware of the danger. "The networks should definitely think of issuing a health warning beforehand," he said. After this incident, several distributers in the U.S. started negotiations to bring **Pokemon** to American television. It was subsequently picked up for domestic syndication, where it has enjoyed tremendous popularity. It is doubtful, however, that the *Computer Warrior Porigon* episode will ever be shown again.

MIND STALKERS

Voices In The Brain

It has been known for some time that the human brain can be influenced by a myriad of outside influences. Yet few people realize that the brain can be manipulated by such things as bright, flashing lights, like the **Pokemon** incident, to microwaves and other "beamed" electronic sources. The stereotypical image of the mentally ill person who complains that the government is beaming messages into their brain, might not be so far-fetched after all.

There were three scientists who pioneered the work of using an electromagnetic field to control human behavior. The three were Dr. Jose Delgado, psychology professor at Yale University. Dr. W. Ross Adey, a physiologist at the Brain Research Institute at UCLA, and Dr. Wilder Penfield, a Canadian. Dr. Jose Delgado was a pioneer of the technology of Electrical Stimulation of the Brain (ESB).

The New York Times ran an article on May 17, 1965 entitled *Matador With a Radio Stops Wild Bull*. The story details Dr. Delgado's experiments at Yale University School of Medicine and work in the field at Cordova, Spain. The article stated:

"Afternoon sunlight poured over the high wooden barriers into the ring, as the brave bull bore down on the unarmed matador, a scientist who had never faced fighting bull. But the charging animal's horn never reached the man behind the heavy red cape. Moments before that could happen, Dr. Delgado pressed a button on a small radio transmitter in his hand and the bull braked to a halt. Then he pressed another button on the transmitter, and the bull obediently turned to the right and trotted away. The bull was obeying commands in his brain that were being called forth by electrical stimulation by the radio signals to certain regions in which fine wires had been painlessly planted the day before."

According to Dr. Delgado, experiments of this type have also been performed on humans. While giving a lecture on the brain in 1965, Dr. Delgado said, "Science has developed a new methodology for the study and control of cerebral function in animals and humans." Dr. Delgado was able to achieve a type of mind control with the assistance of a device he named a "stimoceiver." This electronic apparatus was the forerunner of the more sophisticated computerized devises that are used today.

MIND STALKERS

Invented in the late '50s early '60s, the stimoceiver is a miniature depth electrode which can receive and transmit electronic signals over FM radio waves. By stimulating a correctly-positioned stimoceiver, an outside operator can wield a surprising degree of control over the subject's responses. Delgado's *Physical Control of the Mind: Toward a Psychocivilized Society*, remains the sole full-length, popularly-written work on intracerebral implants and electronic stimulation of the brain (ESB).

While subsequent work has long since superceded the techniques described in this book, Delgado's achievements were far-reaching. His animal and human experiments clearly proved that the experimenter can electronically induce emotions and behavior. Under certain conditions, the extremes of temperament, rage, lust, fatigue, etc., can be easily elicited by an outside operator.

Delgado writes, "Radio stimulation of different points in the amygdala and hippocampus in the four patients produced a variety of effects, including pleasant sensations, elation, deep, thoughtful concentration, odd feelings, super relaxation, colored visions, and other responses."

In a fascinating series of experiments, Delgado attached the stimoceiver to the tympanic membrane, thereby transforming the ear into a sort of microphone. An assistant would whisper "How are you?" into the ear of a "fitted" cat, and Delgado could hear the words over a loudspeaker in the next room. The application of this technology to the spy trade should be readily apparent.

According to Victor Marchetti, The Agency once attempted a highly sophisticated extension of this basic idea, in which radio implants were attached to a cat's cochlea, to facilitate the pinpointing of specific conversations, freed from extraneous surrounding noises. By the 1970's this technique had been throughly developed and allegedly made operational with thousands of people being unknowingly "fixed" with stimoceiver's, many of these unwilling victims were left with false memories of "alien abductions."

Dr. Penfield's experiments consisted of the implantation of electrodes deep into the cortexes of epilepsy patients who were to undergo surgery. Penfield was able to drastically improve the memories of these patients through electrical stimulation.

MIND STALKERS

Dr. Adey implanted transmitters in the brains of cats and chimpanzees that could send signals to a receiver regarding the electrical activity of the brain. Additional radio signals were sent back into the brains of the animals which modified their behavior at the direction of the doctor.

Other experiments using platinum, gold and stainless steel electrode implants enabled researchers to induce total madness in cats, put monkeys into a stupor, or to set human beings jerking their arms up and down. Much of Delgado's work was financed by the CIA through phony funding conduits masking themselves as charitable organizations.

Following the successes of Delgado's work, the CIA set up their own research program in the field of electromagnetic behavior modification under the code name Sleeping Beauty. Under the guidance of Dr. Ivor Browning, a laboratory was set up in New Mexico, specializing in working with the hypothalamus in the brain. Here it was found that stimulating this area could produce intense euphoria.

Dr. Browning was able to wire a radio receiver-amplifier into the hypothalamus of a donkey which picked up a five-micro-amp signal, such that he could create intense happiness in the animal. Using the jolts of happiness as an "electronic carrot," Browning was able to send the donkey up a 2000 foot New Mexico mountain and back to its point of origin. When the donkey was going up the path toward its destination, it was rewarded, when it deviated, the signal stopped. "You've never seen a donkey so eager to keep on course in your whole life," Dr. Browning exclaimed. There was a move within the CIA to conduct further experiments on humans, foreigners and prisoners, but officially the White House vetoed the idea as unethical. It is believed that further research continued despite official denial.

Electromagnetic Interrogation

In May 1989, it was learned by the CIA that the KGB was subjecting people undergoing interrogation to electromagnetic fields, which produced a panic reaction, bringing them closer to breaking down under questioning. The subjects were not told that they were being placed under the influence of these beams. A few years earlier, Dr. Ross Adey released photographs and a fact sheet concerning what he called the Russian Lida machine. This consisted of a small transmitter emitting 10-hertz waves which make the subject susceptible to hypnotic suggestion. American POWs in Korea have said that similar devices had been used for interrogation purposes in POW camps.

The general, long term goal of the CIA experiments was to find out whether mind control could be achieved through the use of a precise, external, electromagnetic beam. The electrical activity of the brain operates within the range of 100 hertz. This spectrum is called ELF or Extremely Low Frequency range.

ELF waves carry very little ionizing radiation and very low heat, and therefore do not manifest gross, observable physical effects on living organisms. Published Soviet experiments with ELFs reveal that there was a marked increase in psychiatric and central nervous system disorders and symptoms of stress for sailors working close to ELF generators.

In the mid-1970s, the United States was extremely interested in combining EMR techniques with hypnosis. Plans were on file to develop these techniques through experiments on human volunteers. The spoken word of a hypnotist could be conveyed by modulated electromagnetic energy directly into the subconscious parts of the human brain. This could be done without the use of any devices on the target, or allow the victim to control the information input consciously.

In California, it was discovered by Dr. Adey that animal brain waves could be altered directly by ELF fields. It was found that monkey brains would fall in phase with ELF waves. These waves could easily pass through the skull, which normally protected the central nervous system from outside influence.

In San Leandro, Dr. Elizabeth Rauscher, director of Technic Research Laboratory, has been doing ELF/brain research with human subjects for some time. She had discovered that certain frequencies can produce nausea for more than an hour. Another frequency, she calls it the marijuana frequency, gets people laughing. "Give me the money and three months," she says, "and I'll be able to affect the behavior of 80 percent of the people in this town without their knowing it."

MIND STALKERS

Secret Russian Microwave Weapons

In the past, the former Soviet Union has invested large sums of time and money investigating microwaves and their possible effect on humans. In 1952, while the Cold War was showing no signs of thawing, there was a secret meeting at the Sandia Corporation in New Mexico between U.S. and Soviet scientists involving the exchange of information regarding the biological hazards and safety levels of EMR. The Soviets possessed the greater preponderance of information, and the American scientists were unwilling to take it seriously. In subsequent meetings, the Soviet scientists continued to stress the seriousness of the risks, while American scientists downplayed their importance.

Shortly after the last Sandia meeting, the Soviets began directing a microwave beam at the U.S. embassy in Moscow, using embassy workers as guinea pigs for low-level EMR experiments. Washington, D.C. was oddly quiet regarding the Moscow embassy bombardment. Discovered in 1962, the Moscow signal was investigated by the CIA, which hired a consultant, Milton Zaret, and code named the research Project Pandora. According to Zaret, the Moscow signal was composed of several frequencies, and was focused precisely upon the Ambassador's office.

The intensity of the bombardment was not made public, but when the State Department finally admitted the existence of the signal, it announced that it was fairly low in intensity. There was a consensus among Soviet EMR researchers that a beam such as the Moscow signal was destined to produced blurred vision and loss of mental concentration. The ***Boston Globe*** reported that the American ambassador had not only developed a leukemia-like blood disease, but also suffered from bleeding eyes and chronic headaches.

Under the CIA's Project Pandora, monkeys were brought into the embassy and exposed to the Moscow signal; they were found to have developed blood composition anomalies and unusual chromosome counts. Embassy personnel were found to have a 40 percent higher than average white blood cell count. While Project Pandora's data gathering continued, embassy personnel continued working in the facility and were not informed of the bombardment until 10 years later. Embassy employees were eventually granted a 20 percent hardship allowance for their service in an unhealthful post.

MIND STALKERS

Throughout the period of bombardment, the CIA used the opportunity to gather data on psychological and biological effects of the beam on American personnel. The U.S. government began to examine the effects of the Moscow signal. The job was turned over to the Defense Advanced Research Projects Agency (DARPA). DARPA is now in the process of developing electromagnetic weaponry.

Navy Captain Dr. Paul E. Taylor read a paper at the Air University Center for Aerospace Doctrine, Research and Education, at Maxwell Air Force Base, Alabama. In his paper, Dr. Taylor stated, "The ability of individuals to function (as soldiers) could be degraded with the use of microwaves to such a point that they would be combat ineffective."

The effects of repeated exposure of microwaves have been repeatedly downplayed by government scientists. The public has not been made aware of the information gathered during Project Pandora of the lethal effects of daily exposure to microwave energy. Something Soviet scientists knew and implemented years ago.

Brain Bombs

Lawrence Livermore National Laboratory was reported to have been involved on the development of a "brain bomb." A bomb that could be dropped in the middle of a battlefield which would produce microwaves, incapacitating the minds of soldiers within a prescribed area. Rumors persist that such a "brain bomb" was secretly used on Iraqi soldiers during the Gulf war, prompting them to drop their weapons and surrender peacefully.

According to a May 1995 program on ARD television in Germany, a "Psychotronic Influence System" developed by the Soviet KGB in the 1970's that turns people into programmable "human weapons" is being used today by the Russian police. The system relies on hypnosis and high-frequency radio waves and can be activated by code words. Psychotronic Influence Systems were first publicized at a conference in Russia sponsored by Gorbachev's Glasnost Foundation. Those programmed included members of the special forces and regular soldiers in the Afghan conflict, which ended in 1988.

MIND STALKERS

Alexander Kutchurov, head of Russia's Institute for Parapsychological Research, said that Psychotronic Influence Systems made its subjects incapable of feeling sympathy. Valery Kaniuka, former project leader, now regrets his role, describing Psychotronic Influence Systems as "the destruction of the human intellect." After the existence of the project was made public, hundreds of former Soviet soldiers, police and KGB members filed for damages, saying they were psychological wrecks with chronic headaches and hallucinations.

According to Yuri Malin, a former Gorbachev security adviser, the Psychotronic Influence Systems project was started in response to a similar training scheme launched in the United States by President Carter. Though Gorbachev halted Psychotronic Influence Systems training in 1988, the technique found its way onto the free market, where mobsters and private security firms are said to be using it. It is also used by special police units before they go into action against drug dealers or demonstrators. This according to the ARD report, which showed footage of police watching a video in which a seated man apparently utters the activating code words.

In September 1990, the **Washington Post** published an article dealing with the growing concern within the United States intelligence community over the Russian's progress in the development of long-range electronic mind control: "According to the communications of Russian defectors, the Russians have succeeded in influencing human behavior, changing human feelings and health condition, incurring unconsciousness and even killing people."

One document from the Intelligence Service at the United States Department of Defense says that the Soviet experiments imposed on the recipient results in, "disquietude combined with short windedness and the feeling of being hit on the head." Some western observers of electronic extra sensorial developments are alarmed by the possible effects of "subconscious influencing when used against the U.S. staff operating nuclear missiles."

The Soviet newspaper **Komsomolskaya Pravda** opened an investigation to find facts verifying these stories. A Russian scientist stated for the newspaper that "it is possible to produce a mind control machine, that the machine would work on bases of electromagnetic waves and that it is not out of question that such a machine is under construction." During the attempted coup in Moscow in August 1991, General Kobec warned the defenders of the Russian White House against the use of Psychotronical weapons.

On August 27, 1991, the **Komsomolskaya Pravda** published a statement by Victor Sedleckij, the Vice President of the League of Independent Soviet Scientists where he commented, "As an expert and juridical personality I declare: In Kiev was launched a mass production of Psychotronical Biogenerators and their tests. I cannot assert that during the coup d'etat were used exactly the Kiev generators. All the same the fact that they were used is evident to me. What are the Psychotronical generators? They are electrical equipment which produces the effect of guided control in human organisms. It affects especially the left and right hemisphere of the cortex. This is also the technology of the U.S. project Zombie 5 . . . I draw on my personal experience since I am myself the designer of such a generator."

After that statement several Russian newspapers reopened their investigation on the matter. This time the number of institutions working on the project (about 20), the budget (half a billion Russian rubles), and the contents of the government document approving of the project were published. Among the unconfirmed information there was a rumor that there exists an agreement among twenty countries that they would not use these devices against each other. There is also good evidence that points to the use of Psychotronical generators against political dissidents and internal terrorist groups.

One scientist also stated that "in order to control human behavior, a complicated computer program and strong transmitter are needed." In February 1994, *Newsweek* wrote "Sources tell *Newsweek* that the FBI consulted Moscow experts on the possible use of a Soviet technique for beaming subliminal messages to David Koresh. The technique was inaudible transmissions that could have convinced Koresh he was hearing the voice of God inside his head."

The **Village Voice** published an interview with Steve Killion, deputy chief of the FBI's technical services division. Killion claimed that in March 1993 "Russian scientists demonstrated to 10 American military, intelligence and law-enforcement officials in Washington, a device they claimed could subliminally implant thoughts in people's minds and thereby control their actions."

MIND STALKERS

Steven Killion stated that he was present at the demonstration and was shown how siege situations could be ended easily. "In the normal course of your negotiation with the individual by telephone you can impress a coded message," said Killion, "it is not realized consciously by the individual, but subconsciously, subliminally, they understand it."

According to the ***Bulletin of the Atomic Scientists*** (September - October 1994) the agreement among 20 countries hinted at in the Russian press and known as the "Inhuman Weapons Convention" really exists. The full name is "Convention on Prohibition or Restriction of the Use of Certain Conventional Weapons Which May be Deemed to be excessively Injurious or to Have Indiscriminate Effects."

The Convention reportedly bans the use of weapons that use "electromagnetic energy" (microwave or radio frequency radiation, pulsed at brain-wave frequency, these weapons are said to cause interference with mental processes, or disruption of internal organ functions). The agreement though fails to address the use of such weapons on the civilian population by their own governments, or against citizens of countries who were not involved in the Inhuman Weapons Convention.

For example, there is a strong possibility that an electronic mind control device was used on November 1986 in Germany. At the opening of the trial with two Arabian terrorists in West Berlin, the two defendants claimed that the Federal Republic of Germany was using psychological torture that was transmitting voices into their paralyzed brains. These voices made the men confess to crimes they did not commit. When the Judge asked how this happened, the men said that some kind of "radio beam" were shot into their heads. The Judge dismissed the defendants claims despite evidence showing an extreme jump in "background" microwaves during the trial.

Applications of microwave technology in espionage have been available for over 25 years. In a meeting in Berkeley of the American Association for the Advancement of Science, as early as 1965, Professor J. Anthony Deutsch of New York University, provided an important segment of research in the field of memory control. Professor Deutsch discovered that the mind is a transmitter, and if too much information is received, the brain ceases to transmit. The Professor showed that an excess of acetyl choline in the brain can interfere with the memory process and control.

MIND STALKERS

Electronic Dissolution Of Memory

Professor Deutsch showed that excess amounts of acetyl choline can be artificially produced, through both the administration of drugs and through the use of radio waves. The process is called Electronic Dissolution of Memory (EDOM). The memory transmission can be stopped for as long as the radio signal continues. As a result, the awareness of the person skips over those minutes during which he is subjected to the radio signal. Memory is distorted, and time-orientation is destroyed.

According to Lincoln Lawrence, author of **Were We Controlled?** (New Hyde Park, NY: University Books, 1967), EDOM is now operational. "There is already in use a small EDOM generator/transmitter which can be concealed on the body of the person. Contact with this person, a casual handshake or even just a touch, transmits a tiny electronic charge plus an ultrasonic signal tone which for a short period will disturb the time-orientation of the person affected . . . it can be a potent weapon for hopelessly confusing evidence in the investigation of a crime."

Thirty five years ago, Allen Frey discovered that microwaves of 300 to 3000 megahertz could be "heard" by people, even if they were deaf, if pulsed at a certain rate. Appearing to be originating just in back of the head, the sound boomed, clicked, hissed or buzzed, depending upon the frequency.

Later research has shown that the perception of the waves takes place just in front of the ears. The microwaves cause pressure waves in the brain tissue, and this phenomenon vibrates the sound receptors in the inner ear through the bone structure. Some microwaves are capable of directly stimulating the nerve cells of the auditory pathways. This has been confirmed with experiments with rats, in which the sound registers 120 decibels, which are equal to the volume of a nearby jet during takeoff.

Besides having the capability of causing pain and preventing auditory communication, a more subtle effect was shown at the Walter Reed Army Institute of Research by Dr. Joseph C. Sharp. Dr. Sharp, himself, was the subject of an experiment in which pulsed microwave audiograms, or the microwave analog of the sound vibrations of spoken words, were delivered to his brain in such a way that he was able to understand the words that were spoken. Military and undercover uses of such a device might include driving a subject crazy with inner voices in order to discredit him, or conveying undetectable instructions to a programmed assassin.

It has been proved by Dr. Ross Adey that microwaves can be used to directly cause changes in the electrical patterns of different parts of the brain. His experiments showed that he could achieve the same mind control over animals as Dr. Delgado did in the bull incident. Dr. Delgado used brain implants in his animals, Dr. Adey used microwave devices without preconditioning. He made animals act and look like electronic toys simply by beaming microwaves directly into certain parts of the brain. Recent criminal cases where an otherwise "normal" person goes berserk and kills indiscriminately, could be the result of beamed microwaves controlling that persons mind. The only question is, why?

Have weapons of this nature been developed and field-tested? Judging by the number of individuals and groups that have come forward with complaints of harassment the answer appears to be yes. In 1986, Kim Besley - of the Greenham Common Women's Peace Camp - compiled a catalogue of symptoms blamed on low frequency signals emanating from the U.S. Greenham Common base and, apparently, targeted on the women protesters.

These include vertigo, retinal bleeding, face burns (even at night), nausea, sleep disturbances, palpitations, loss of concentration, loss of memory, disorientation, severe headaches, temporary paralysis, faulty speech coordination, irritability and a sense of panic in non-panic situations. Identical effects have been reported elsewhere and appear to be fairly commonplace among victims. Many of these symptoms have been associated in medical literature with exposure to microwave and especially low intensity or nonthermal exposures. These incidents may be the precursor to future crowd control by microwave.

Some have speculated that there is a secret attempt to control the population by using the fear of crime. Certain individuals are selected, their minds are controlled by any number of methods that has been developed. These controlled people are then influenced to commit crimes and instill fear in the general population. The authorities then are able to gain more control under the guise of a "war on crime."

CHAPTER SIX

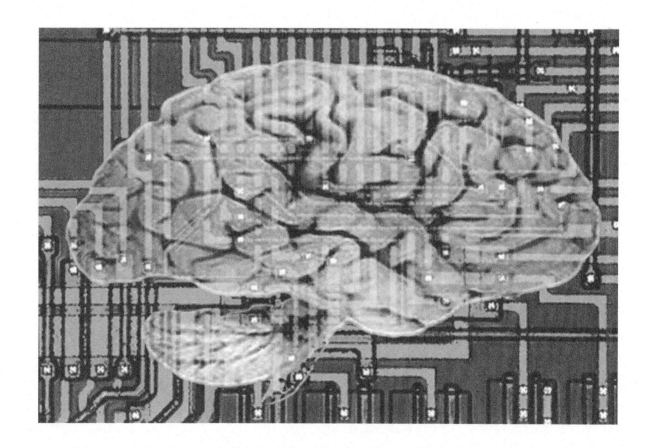

THE MIND MACHINES

MIND STALKERS

These electronic skull zappers are designed to invade the mind and short-circuit its synapses. In the hands of government technicians it may be used to disorient entire crowds or to manipulate individuals into self destructive acts. It's a terrifying weapon.

Dr. Emery Horvath
Harvard professor of physics
commenting on the use of
electromagnetic generators
that interfere with human brain waves

MIND STALKERS

The world has always been a violent place. Over uncountable generations, mankind as a species had to face the fact that aggressive behavior seems to be hardwired into the most primitive parts of the human brain. Despite the fact that humans have developed moral and religious constraints, the beast within will not be stilled. There are still moments of such extreme violence and depravity that one has to wonder how far from the animals have we really come.

The end of the twentieth century has seen a number of violent crimes committed by people who seemingly had no previous violent tendencies. This type of crime has become so common that the term "going postal" has become synonymous with someone suddenly erupting into murderous behavior.

An especially disturbing trend is the increasing number of incidents involving children taking guns to school. Many of these cases have ended in the tragic deaths of fellow students and teachers. While some of the perpetrators have had a history of antisocial behavior, a surprising number of others have absolutely no past evidence of being capable of initiating such mind- bending horrors.

Because of these kinds of unexplained crimes, some researchers have uncovered evidence of research and development of several different types of mind control initiatives. The very real possibility exists that certain kinds of criminal activity could actually be artificially induced by some unknown outside party. The implications are staggering. The questions, however, remain. How and why would anyone want to conduct such a evil and detrimental program?

Critics claim that mind control operations are impossible. However, if this were true, then why have there been numerous secret programs over the years to research and develop such a possibility? In July 1977, The *New York Times* reported on a fourteen-year program by the CIA to control human behavior with drugs, electric shock, radiation, ultrasonic waves, psychology and psychosurgery.

Have years of clandestine research into human mind manipulation finally achieved the unthinkable? Does there now exist a technology that can enable the human brain to be unknowingly controlled from a distance? A "white paper" published in 1991 by the U.S. Global Strategy Council, a Washington - based organization, under the chairmanship of Ray Cline, former Deputy Director of the CIA, describes the

MIND STALKERS

foreign and domestic uses foreseen for laser weapons, isotropic radiators, infra-sound, non-nuclear electromagnetic pulse generators, and high-powered microwave emitters.

Voices In Your Head

In 1961, Allen Frey, a freelance biophysicist and engineering psychologist, reported that humans can hear microwaves. This discovery was dismissed by most United States scientists as the result of outside noise.

A more technical description of the experiment is described by James C. Linn. "Frey found that human subjects exposed to 1310 MHz and 2982 MHz microwaves at average power densities of 0.4 to 2 mW/cm2 perceived auditory sensations described as buzzing or knocking sounds. The sensation occurred instantaneously at average incident power densities well below that necessary for known biological damage and appeared to originate from within or near the back of the head."

Two researchers by the names of Joseph Sharp and Mark Grove performed experiments in which audible voices were sent by microwaves directly to the brain. A recording of someone speaking the number's one through ten was first used in the experiment. The electrical sine wave analogs of each word were processed so that each time a sine wave crossed zero reference in the negative direction, a brief pulse of microwave energy was triggered. By radiating themselves with these voice-modulated microwaves, Sharp and Grove were readily able to hear, identify, and distinguish among the nine words. The sounds heard were not unlike those emitted by persons with artificial larynxes.

Dr. James Lin of Wayne State University has written a book entitled: *Microwave Auditory Effects and Applications*. It explores the possible mechanisms for the phenomenon, and discusses possibilities for the deaf, as persons with certain types of hearing loss can still hear pulsed microwaves (as tones or clicks and buzzes, if words aren't modulated on). Lin mentions the Sharp and Grove experiment and comments: "The capability of communicating directly with humans by pulsed microwaves is obviously not limited to the field of therapeutic medicine."

MIND STALKERS

Dr. Robert O. Becker, twice nominated for the Noble prize for his health work in bio-electromagnetism, was more explicit in his concern over illicit government activity. He wrote of "obvious application in covert operations designed to drive a target crazy with voices."

What is frightening is that words, transmitted via low density microwaves or radio frequencies, or by other covert methods, might be used to create influence. For instance, according to a 1984 U.S. House of Representatives report, a large number of stores throughout the country use high frequency transmitted words (above the range of human hearing) to discourage shoplifting. Stealing is reported to be reduced by as much as 80 percent in some cases.

With the use of computers, the process to "broadcast" complex messages directly into a subjects brain must by now be a relatively simple task. People who call themselves "wavies" say that this is precisely what is happening to them on a daily basis. Wavies claim that they are the victims of "electronic harassment" that radiates voices in their heads. They assert that the CIA and the Defense Department are engaged in a highly selective and effective project of directed-energy mind control experimentation. They call it microwave harassment.

The complaints of microwave harassment are chilling. Their uncompromising tone and lack of corroborating evidence quickly leads one to dismiss them as paranoid rants. Conspiracy literature flourishes with microwave mind control stories. Analysis of the literature finds only tantalizing hints that the technology of high-quality audiogram transmission is real.

In 1975, researcher A. W. Guy stated that "one of the most widely observed and accepted biologic effects of low average power electromagnetic energy is the auditory sensation evoked in man when exposed to pulsed microwaves."

He concluded that at frequencies where the auditory effect can be easily detected, microwaves penetrate deep into the tissues of the head, causing rapid thermal expansion (at the microscopic level only) which produces strains in the brain tissue.

MIND STALKERS

An acoustic stress wave is then conducted through the skull to the cochlea, and from there, it proceeds in the same manner as in conventional hearing. It is obvious that receiver-less radio has not been adequately publicized or explained because of national security concerns.

Those that do attempt to publicize such research, or try to investigate Wavie complaints are often targeted with harassment themselves. Dr. Elizabeth Rauscher recalls the forces of resistance that came from her efforts to delve into the mysterious world of mind control victims.

"In trying to help these people. I got in tremendous trouble. I was told by some people in Washington that I could not publish my research that I funded with my own money at my own place and I was told I would be blackballed if I did. At the time I did not report much of what I did, but I was blackballed anyway! I am thinking to myself 'This is crazy! Where is the Constitution in this thing?'"

Today, the ability to remotely transmit microwave voices inside a target's head is known inside the Pentagon as "Synthetic Telepathy." According to Dr. Robert Becker, "Synthetic Telepathy has applications in covert operations designed to drive a target crazy with voices or deliver undetected instructions to a programmed assassin."

This technology may have contributed to the deaths of 25 defense scientists variously employed by Marconi Underwater and Defense Systems, Easems and GEC. Most of the scientists worked on highly sensitive electronic warfare programs for NATO, including the Strategic Defense Initiative. It is claimed that directed energy weapons may have been used to literally drive these men to suicide and 'accidents.' For what reason would any government, military or intelligence agency subject innocent people to clandestine mind control attempts? If such a program is being conducted then the overall cost must amount in the billions of dollars yearly. For such a budget, the secret mind control operation must be extremely important to someone. The chilling answer could be that some group is in the process of creating an army of secret assassins using remote mind control technology. The system is so secret that not even the assassins themselves know that they have been programmed to be killers when the need arises.

MIND STALKERS

The Mind Reading Machine

Alan Yu, a former lieutenant colonel in the Taiwan National Defense Department, says that the United States has not only developed an operational mind control machine, but has also distributed models for use by allied countries. Yu states that such machines pose a great threat to human rights and the American way of life. He calls the device the "Mind Reading Machine" (Mind Machine).

Yu writes that there are two sources of information detailing the existence of the Mind Reading Machine. The first evidence: In the 1970s, *The South China Morning Post* reported that the University of Maryland had invented a thought reading machine. The original purpose of this invention was to help authorities investigate severe car accidents. It was meant to be used on people who were severely injured to get their accounts of how the accidents occurred. The CIA quickly learned of this invention and reportedly purchased the patent.

In the spring of 1984, Yu was a lieutenant colonel serving in the National Defense Department of Taiwan. At that time, Yu read a classified document from the department that he serviced under. The document said the Military Police Department of Taiwan had purchased several of the Mind Reading machines from the United States (In Taiwan, it was called Psychological Language Machine).

The document was a request to the United States for parts to repair several malfunctioning machines. The machine allegedly uses microwaves to deliver spoken messages directly to the human brain, as well as using radio waves to hypnotize people or change their thoughts. Yu reports that before he left this machine had become the most effective weapon for the security departments of Taiwan.

Insane In The Brain

In the 1970's and 80's it was widely believed by certain religious and political groups that rock music was being used to transmit subliminal messages to their listeners. The music supposedly had hidden "backward masked" commands, usually urging allegiance to Satan and then suicide.

MIND STALKERS

Lawsuits were filed against several "heavy metal" bands by parents of teenagers who killed themselves after listening to albums produced by the groups. Lawyers for the bands pointed out that it would make little financial sense for the bands to try and "kill off" the very people who were buying their albums. The juries agreed and all cases brought to trial ended in favor of the bands.

There could, however, be some truth to the "hidden messages" scenario. However, instead of rock albums having backward masked commands, other, more subtle ways exist to silently program an individual or group to perform acts of violence.

In 1993, *Defense News* announced that the Russian government was discussing with American counterparts the transfer of technical information and equipment known as "Acoustic Psycho-correction." The Russians claimed that this device involves the transmission of specific commands via static or white noise bands into the human subconscious without upsetting other intellectual functions.

Demonstrations of this equipment have shown encouraging results after exposure of less than one minute and have produced the ability to alter behavior on unwilling subjects. A US Department of Defense medical engineer claimed in 1989 that the U.S. and Israel had regularly used microwaves to condition and control the minds of Palestinians.

Given the low power levels required for some of these psycho-physical effects, and the ability to concentrate certain frequencies of electromagnetic radiation into tight beams, it is worth considering the possibility that low-orbiting satellites could transmit such signals directly to a chosen person. Such a capability would have obvious strategic value.

What If?

What if some group or organization wanted to conduct terrorist activities that would strike right into the heart of their intended victims? What better way than to create killers from the most ordinary of citizens? Worse yet would be to cause children to unexpectedly lash out and murder those around them. It is apparent that the tech -

nology exists to elicit such behavior using waves of electromagnetic energy sent directly into the brain. The question remains though who would to do such a thing, and why?

Considering the expenses of such a terror campaign being waged on the citizens of the planet, the most likely suspects would be the government or military. Another possibility would be a rogue group within the intelligence or military communities.

Sally Freeland, who says she has been harassed by mind control activities, is certain that her tormenters are simply "criminals" who have enough money to buy easily produced mind control technology. Freeland's theory might not be so far-fetched. Just about any science or electronics magazine will have at least one, if not more, advertisement selling plans for "mind control" machines.

It should also be considered that "silent commands to kill" are not intended for anyone in general. Whoever is unlucky enough to be able to "pick up" the message and react to it after a length of time would serve a terrorist agenda quite satisfactory. In fact, so much the better. Those who can pick up the signals with their minds would probably be already inclined toward some kinds of violent behavior. It is then a simple task to send the "kill command" to an already compliant mind. That way, when the carnage is over, the media can report on how the sick individual had shown previous warning signs that everyone ignored.

Even if such events are not random acts of violence, and even if these people are being mentally controlled by an outside source, the question is still, why? A terrorist campaign is successful only if those being terrorized know their attackers. So far, the mind controllers have not stepped forward to make their demands known. Because of this, the chilling scenario that we are in the midst of a larger political goal bent on the eventual control and containment of the free people of planet Earth might be plausible.

CHAPTER SEVEN

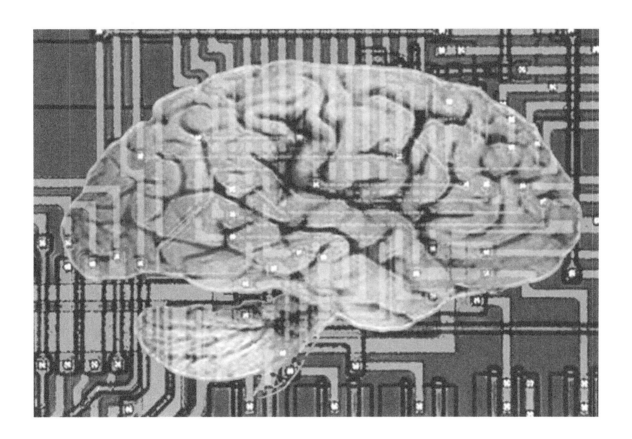

THE UFO CONNECTION

MIND STALKERS

The mind of a person coming out of fairyland is usually blank as to what has been seen and done there.

Walter Wentz,
The Fairy Faith in Celtic Countries

MIND STALKERS

The idea of mind control by the government or clandestine groups is in itself a disturbing concern. Yet the possibility that humans are being mentally manipulated by extraterrestrial intelligence's is a scenario far more horrifying to contemplate.

A number of investigators have suspected that UFOs may be responsible for somehow controlling the minds of some witnesses and abductees. UFO literature is filled with hundreds of cases in which observers have been subjected to continuous harassments following an encounter with a UFO. Some witnesses report strange, ghost-like phenomena in their homes. In other cases, weird, mechanical-sounding voices, purported to be "messages" from extraterrestrials, begin emanating from their phones, radios and televisions.

Some witnesses persist in believing that they are being harassed controlled day and night by UFO entities. Cases of UFO mind manipulation are actually quite common. Yet very little is known about it because of the scant research being conducted. Investigators have attempted to distance themselves from cases of alien mind control. Most feel that the witnesses who complain of such attacks are probably mentally ill. However, the research that has been done shows that accounts of UFO mind control are almost always identical.

The pattern that emerges usually follows a close encounter with a UFO. The eyewitness goes through a period of anxiety, during which he is unable to consciously remember certain aspects of the incident. Within months, the personality of the observer actually changes. Eventually, it may change to the point where he finds it impossible to get along with co-workers, friends or even family. Personal tragedy seems to strike many of those who have had UFO experiences.

In some cases, the eyewitness discovers he has developed certain "gifts" or abilities. Though they may appear to be beneficial at first, too often this is not the case. Among these unusual abilities are powers of ESP, precognition, or psychokinesis. In addition, a heightened intelligence level or an unusual increase in physical strength may be noticed. Such peculiarities will often manifest themselves shortly before a person is about to be controlled. Shortly after this, he may begin slipping into a "trance," during which time it appears as if an alien intelligence has "taken over" his body and is using his brain.

MIND STALKERS

There are hundreds of so-called "mental contactees" who claim to receive information and data of a highly advanced scientific and philosophical nature. During the 1950's and 60's, this method of communicating with UFO occupants (better known as channeling) became so popular that entities calling themselves "Ashtar," "Agar," and "Monka" were heard from daily, somewhere in the world.

There is no doubt that this phenomenon is widespread and it is by no means limited to the United States. Cases of mind-altering UFOs seem to be occurring at an alarming rate. There have been reports of entire communities being placed under a strange "spell," with the simultaneous appearance of UFOs in the area.

Mental Invaders

A large-scale attempt to invade and seize the minds of human beings occurred on April 29, 1967, when a coastal village on the outskirts of Rio de Janeiro became the target of a mysterious malady that may have been perpetrated by a strange craft sighted overhead.

For about one hour on that day, the citizens of Barra de Tijuca, Brazil, were literally forced into establishing contact with an unearthly intelligence, which quickly subdued many people in the town. The series of disturbing events began at noon, when an emergency telephone call reached Dr. Jeronemo Rodrigues Morales, chief physician at Barr de Tijuca's general hospital. An excited voice explained how a man in his late 60s had fallen unconscious on the beach near town.

Dr. Morales immediately drove to the scene. Upon arriving he found the man brushing sand from his clothes and talking to a crowd of people who had gathered to offer help. "I was merely walking about the sand dunes," the man explained. "I had been watching the gulls high above the water, when suddenly I blacked out."

An examination ruled out the possibility of a heart attack and Dr. Morales decided that the man had suffered a mild case of sunstroke. Within minutes, another call came in with the news that a fisherman had been discovered in shallow water beneath a nearby bridge, and was said to be trembling from shock.

MIND STALKERS

Dr. Morales quickly drove to the area and arrived just in time to see the "stricken" fisherman casually drying himself off, and asking what all the excitement was about. When the doctor explained that he had blacked out, the man seemed insulted. "I'm not sick," he argued. "I feel perfectly well." He assured Dr. Morales that he had been tossing his nets into these waters every day for twenty years without any difficulty, and would do so for twenty more.

Within a short while, Dr. Morales received word of six other "stricken" individuals. All followed the identical pattern: People keeling over, then reviving themselves without aid, and, after a flurry of excitement, insisting that nothing was wrong.

While Dr. Morales was treating a mother and her young son, both who had collapsed together on the beach, he noticed something high overhead. Glistening in the sun, the doctor observed an enormous disc-shaped UFO over the town. The craft was darting about in the sky at tremendous speeds. Several other physicians and nurses on the hospital staff reported that they had seen the UFO suspended over the town since noon. Shortly after that, the object disappeared along with the strange illness. Still, the town's people had not heard the last from their strange visitor. Three days later, another UFO, similar to the first, appeared over the city. Once more, a number of people dropped unconscious to the ground. During these two days, many other individuals were treated at the hospital for headaches and dizziness. Some even reported hearing strange voices talking to them in an unknown language.

Voices From The Sky

In the weeks after the strange incident at Barra de Tijuca, people who had experienced the mysterious malady began to speak openly about what happened to them. Most reported a strange voice in their head that spoke in a guttural language no one understood. Others said the voice was clearly understandable and kept repeating the phrase "do not be afraid" over and over. One man said the voice told him not to tell anyone what had happened to him, and promised that it would return soon. What has not been reported are the continuing strange incidents that have plagued many of the town's people of Barra de Tijuca in the years after their initial event.

MIND STALKERS

One Brazilian UFO investigator wrote that: "The people of Barra de Tijuca continue to be haunted by the insistent voices in their heads. Most will no longer talk to outsiders about their problems. Those that do tell frighteningly similar stories of voices that control every aspect of their daily lives. The voices, the towns people say, originate from alien beings hovering high overhead in their UFOs."

While some people say that they have learned to "tune out" the constant chatter in their heads, others have not been so fortunate. The suicide rate in town is staggering. Some try to drown out the voices with drugs or alcohol. Others try and leave Barra de Tijuca for good. Nothing really seems to work against the continuing torment. Strangely enough, when asked what the voices talk about, most town people say they can't remember, that the voices didn't want them to remember.

Could there be other towns across the globe experiencing the same harassment? Are the inhabitants of these towns being prepared through mind control for some kind of unknown situation or mission in the future? Might we be faced someday with an army of hypnotically controlled humans, ready through years of mental manipulation, to do the bidding of their otherworldly controllers? In his book **Passport to Magonia**, Jacques Vallee writes of a chilling account of possible alien mind control in the former Soviet Union. "In 1971, an eminent scientist in the field of plasma research, died under suspicious circumstances, he was murdered by a mentally disturbed woman who pushed him into the path of a train at the Moscow subway station. The accused women claimed that a 'voice' from space had instructed her to kill this particular man, and she felt unable to resist the order."

Vallee has also stated that he has heard from "trustworthy sources" that Russian police are disturbed about the recent increase in cases of this nature. "Quite often," Vallee maintains, "mentally unstable people are known to run wildly across a street, protesting they are being pursued by Martians, but the present wave of mental troubles is an aspect of the UFO problem that deserves special attention . . . "

Ukrainian UFO researcher Anton A. Anfalow reports that after the fall of the former Soviet Union, dozens of UFO research groups sprung up in an attempt to finally investigate the thousands of UFO reports that had been suppressed by the government.

MIND STALKERS

Because of their efforts, many prominent researchers soon found themselves being harassed and physically attacked by unknown assailants. These assailants would often act like muggers, but would then forego easier prey to target UFO investigators.

One such attack led to the murder of well-known Russian scientist and UFOlogist Dr. A. Zolotov. Dr. Zolotov was attacked by a knife-wielding stranger in the town of Tver. Russian authorities say that the attacks are being carried out by individuals suffering from a "type of mental illness where the person claims that voices from alien beings are ordering them to kill certain people." Cases such as this have led some to speculate that the wave of alleged abductions of humans is part of an agenda by extraterrestrials to control mankind with the help of electronic implants.

Alien Implants

In recent years, hundreds of people claiming to have had contact with aliens also believe they have been implanted with strange electronic devices. The exact purpose of these microchip-like implants, reportedly found embedded in the skin of abductees, remains unknown. Until recently their existence has only been supported by anecdotal evidence. However, as the abduction phenomenon gathers momentum, more physical evidence is being gathered and studied by doctors and scientists.

According to UFO folklore, implants are usually located in the nasal cavity. In some famous cases, such as the alleged abduction of author Whitley Streiber, brain scans have shown disturbances in an area of the brain close to that part of the body. Some abductees have reported experiencing nose bleeds, believing that implants were forced into their nostrils so that their brains could be monitored and controlled.

In recent years, however, implants have begun appearing in different parts of the body, sometimes in the back of the neck, behind an ear or in the hands and feet. Hard evidence of purported alien technology has been very hard to come by. On August 19, 1995, Ventura, California surgeon Dr. Roger Leir and his surgical team, along with Houston alien contact investigator and Certified Hypnotherapist Derrel Sims, removed three "implants" from two people, a man and a woman who had experienced what they believed to be UFO related incidents in their life.

MIND STALKERS

Two of the implants were removed from the woman's toes. The third was in the back of the man's hand. All three were attached to nerves where no nerves are known to exist. So far, two additional surgeries have been performed. Three out of four patients turned out to have nearly identical, highly anomalous iron alloy objects involved.

In all cases, ultra hard metallic highly magnetic "cores" were surrounded by an ultra dense dark gray membrane which couldn't be cut with a brand-new scalpel. The membrane somehow prevented any sign of inflammation or rejection. Dr. Leir says "If the implants can teach us how to prevent tissue rejection, we could revolutionize surgery."

Interestingly, the membranes on these objects turned out to be made of a tough matrix of proteins from skin and blood. This could explain why the body accepted the objects so readily. It might also explain the very common "scoop marks" that abductees often find on their bodies.

The removed tissue could be wrapped around an implant to "fool" the body into believing the object is part of the system. Also not so easily explained is how the implants got into these people's bodies. Even with a powerful magnifying glass, Dr. Leir could find no sign of a scar or other evidence of a point of entry for objects which had come to be placed deep in the victims tissues.

If implants are actually electronic devices of some kind, the question is: "what is their purpose?" The most prevalent explanation for implants is that they are used to tag an individual to make sure they can be found again. Others believe that the implants are bugging devices, used to monitor conversations and actions. Another theory is that the implants are a means of mentally controlling human subjects. Often, victims of UFO abduction complain of the feeling that their minds are being influenced by aliens. Abductees report a number of experiences that could be induced by the implants: Buzzing, beeping and strange voices, missing time, inexplicable emotions in inappropriate circumstances, loss of self control and telepathic communication. Many report the disturbance of electrical objects in their presence, perhaps a side effect of such implant technologies.

MIND STALKERS

The Purpose Of Implants

In an e-mail letter received by the author, a group who refers to themselves as "The Light," states that people worldwide have been implanted with devices to allow certain kinds of control by extraterrestrial entities. Some of the methods referred to by "The Light" sounds similar to the events described by the late Philip K. Dick.

"Extraterrestrials are currently living among us as humans to monitor human development and assist mankind. Through metabolism cloning, they have the capability to transform their body into a human form taking several minutes. By choosing a desired path, they discreetly & consciously live under a human guise among people without revealing their identity until the correct time. Before society can accept the alien presence, it's culture and organization must be changed, which is why they form an influential global network responsible for waves of UFO and alien phenomenon. These part alien/part-human individuals or hybrid-aliens are called 'Guardians.' The Guardians have been selectively breed with humans over the millenniums in order to produce spiritually evolved beings.

"Alien races have visited the earth for thousands of years for different purposes, but the explanation behind the majority of abductions is that alien beings based on earth are implementing a program to implant selected individuals with technically advanced information to condition, educate, and improve humanity. Across the globe and after an examination period, these people were chosen because of specific traits these beings were comfortable with. This microscopic implant, which lies dormant, is inserted into the brain through a condensed light source or manually using surgical instruments.

"The implant contains the foundation for understanding basic extraterrestrial knowledge, principles, and concepts. Very simple examples include: cures for diseases, undiscovered power sources, formulas for food processing and growing, applications of light, utilization of crystals, etc. The power of advanced knowledge will become second nature without ever affecting the implantees personality and memory. The process of learning has been condensed in a microscopic implant: all the chosen will have a sudden interest in an area that they never had previously as if an extraterrestrial course has been studied. This knowledge will be permanent, even if the implant is surgically removed. There are parts of the human brain that naturally becomes a 'biological storage area' for the information stored in the implants.

"A guide is free to scan any field of interest he or she desires. After implantation, these people are called "Implantees." After the implant is unlocked, these individuals are called Guides.' The Formation is the global event that will simultaneously notify and gather the selected implantees and activate or unlock the implants. The crucial conditioning period after The Formation is called 'The Convergence.'

"The implant also acts as a tracking device in order for the movements of each implantee to be occasionally monitored by a Guardian in close proximity. Through this means, each person will be protected and prevented from an unnatural death. Prior to The Formation, each implantee, regardless of what he or she is doing, will be confronted and informed in detail by a Guardian either verbally or telepathically of what is about to take place. Simultaneously across the world in different countries, all implantees will be transported by means of small crafts to larger crafts situated above the earth. Here the implantee is free to mingle and converse with others across the globe who have been selected, which may or may not include past acquaintances.

"Demonstrations will be given, there will be freedom to interact with hybrid-aliens, and virtually all questions will be answered. Sometime during this period, the implant will be activated or 'unlocked' via a harmless fine-tuning light directed at each persons head, leaving a small red mark for several days. The Convergence has now commenced: the great transformation and advancement these extraterrestrials have been guiding humanity toward. The Guides are now ready to introduce revolutionary and innovative ideas to mankind. For the first time in history, there will be a direct relationship between alien knowledge and society."

Contactees - Or Alien Mind Control Victims?

The UFO phenomenon is complex and offers no easy answers. On one side UFOs appear to be physical, constructed machines, flown by creatures who claim to be from other planets. On the other side is the unphysical nature of the phenomena, with UFOs and the strange beings associated with them manifesting like ghosts.

MIND STALKERS

People who are unlucky enough to get caught up in the confusing world of UFOs and their occupants are often subjected to weird forms of possession, behavioral changes and mind control. Victims of UFO abduction usually report periods of "missing time" which is almost certainly achieved with some kind of mental manipulation of the abductee.

Fortean researcher and author John Keel, speculates that the contactee syndrome is a fundamental reprogramming process. No matter what frame of reference is being used, the experience usually begins with either the sudden flash of light or a sound - a humming, buzzing or beeping. The subject's attention is riveted to a pulsing, flickering light of dazzling intensity. He finds he is unable to move a muscle and is rooted to the spot.

Next the flickering light goes through a series of color changes and a seemingly physical object begins to take form. The light diminishes revealing a UFO, or an entity of some sort. What is really happening is that the percipient is first entranced by the flickering light. From the moment he feels paralyzed, he loses touch with reality and begins to hallucinate. The light remains a light, but the contactees mind is hypnotized to see a spaceship and/or a strange alien creature.

Keel writes in his book, *The Mothman Prophecies*, that he was concerned with the falsified memories of the contactees. "I wondered what happened to the bodies of these people while their minds were taking trips in flying saucers. Trips that often lasted for hours, even for days."

A young college professor in New York State was haunted by the same question in 1967. After investigating a UFO-related poltergeist case, he suffered possession and was led to believe that he had committed a daring jewel robbery while he was in a trance or possessed state. He abandoned Ufology and nearly suffered a total nervous breakdown in the aftermath.

Are contactees and abduction victims being used by exterior intelligence's to carry out crimes, even murder? The answer is a disturbing yes. If you review the history of political assassinations you will find that many were performed by so-called religious fanatics who were obeying the "voice of God," or were in an obvious state of possession when they committed their crime. Assassins such as Sirhan Sirhan, who murdered Robert Kennedy, had a strange fascination with the occult and hypnosis. It is not unusual for them to say that they have no recollection of committing the crime. A telltale indication of mind control.

In contactee parlance, persons who perform involuntary acts are said to be "used." A contactee may feel a sudden impulse to go for a pointless late-night walk or drive. During that drive he encounters, he thinks, the space people and is abducted. Actually his body goes on to, say, Point A where he picks up a letter or object left there by another contactee. He carries the letter or object to Point B and deposits it. Later he has no memories of these actions.

Alien Abductions Or Military Experiments?

According to Helmut Lammer Ph.D., UFO abductions are generally a very complex phenomena. For skeptics, journalists and the public, it is difficult to believe that abductions by alien beings have their basis in physical reality. However, well-respected researchers have shown that the core of the UFO abduction phenomenon cannot be explained psychologically as hallucinations or mass delusions. Recently, some UFO abductees have reported that they have also been kidnaped by military intelligence personnel and taken to hospitals and/or military facilities, some of which are described as being underground.

Very few books on the subject of UFO abductions have mentioned these experiences. Especially disconcerting is the fact that abductees recall seeing military intelligence personnel together with alien beings, working side by side in these secret facilities. Researchers in the field of mind control suggest that these cases are evidence that the whole UFO abduction phenomenon is staged by the intelligence community as a cover for their illegal experiments. Could the whole abduction scenario be a carefully manipulated hypnotic cover for experimentation by government or military
intelligence services?

The alleged military involvement in the abduction phenomenon could be evidence that the military uses abductees for mind control experiments as test-targets for microwave weapons. Moreover, the military could be monitoring and even kidnaping abductees for information gathering purposes during, before and after a UFO abduction.

Lammer's research suggests that abductees are often harassed by dark, unmarked helicopters that fly around their houses. The mysterious helicopter activity goes back to the late sixties and early seventies, when they showed an apparent interest in animal mutilations, but not in alleged UFO abductees. However, UFO researcher Raymond E. Fowler reported some helicopter activity in connection with UFO witnesses during the seventies.

Many abductees report interaction with military intelligence personnel after the helicopters begin to appear. Debbie Jordan reports, for instance, in a side note of her book ***Abducted!***, while she was with a friend, she was kidnaped, drugged and taken to a kind of military hospital where she was examined by a medical doctor. This doctor told her he was going to remove a "bug" from her ear and proceeded to take out an implant that resembled a BB. The abduction experiences of Leah Haley and Katharina Wilson also include military-type encounters. Some of Katharina Wilson's experiences are reminiscent of reported mind control experiments. For example, she writes of a flashback from her childhood where she remembers being forced into what appeared to be a Skinner Box that may have been used for behavior modification purposes. In some military abduction cases military doctors searched for implants and sometimes even implanted the abductee with what appeared to be a man-made implant.

The technology does exist for small, radio frequency electronic implants. More than three million animals worldwide have been successfully implanted with a transponder manufactured by Destron-Fearing. The transponder is a passive radio frequency identification tag, designed to work in conjunction with a compatible radio-frequency ID reading system.

The transponder is activated by a low-frequency radio signal. It then transmits the ID code to the reading system. The smallest transponder is about the size of an uncooked grain of rice. The transponder's tiny electronic circuit is energized by the low-power radio beam sent by a compatible reading device.

MIND STALKERS

A similar bio-chip for humans was patented in 1989 by Dr. Daniel Man. The homing device, which can be implanted under the skin, was originally developed to locate missing children. This device is slightly larger than the Destron implant and a small surgical incision must be made for it to be implanted. Dr. Man claims that the best location for his implant may be behind the ear.

It is possible that some of the information received from abductees may be cover stories, induced by hypno-programming techniques of military psychiatrists. It is also possible that the military uses rubber alien masks and special effects during a supposed alien abduction. Katharina Wilson reported flashbacks where she remembered holding a rubber mask of an alien head in her hands. Facts such as these lead some mind control researchers to believe that all alien abductees are actually mind control and/or genetic experiments staged by a secret group within the government of the United States.

In a declassified memo dated February 17, 1994, former Naval Intelligence Commander Scott Jones, Ph.D. wrote to White House Presidential Science Advisor John Gibbons: "Whatever Roswell turns out to be, it is only the opening round. I urge you to take another look at the UFO Matrix of Belief that I provided you last year. My mention of mind-control technology at the February 4 meeting was quite deliberate.

Please be careful about this. There are reasons to believe that some governmental group has interwoven research about this [mind-control] technology with alleged UFO phenomena. If that is correct, you can expect to run into early resistance when inquiring about UFOs, not because of the UFO subject, but because that has been used to cloak research and applications of mind-control activity."

CHAPTER EIGHT

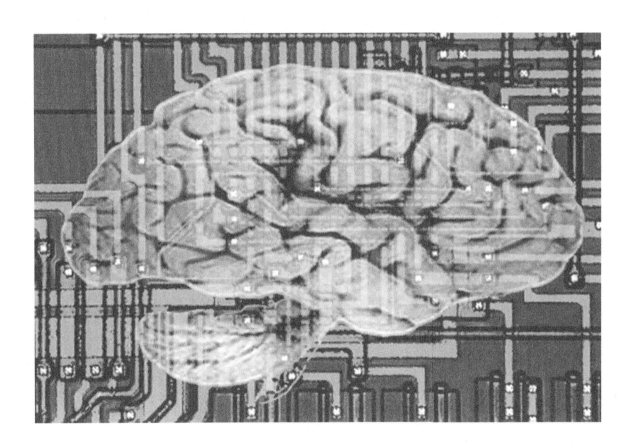

MENTAL ARMAGEDDON:
THE VICTIMS SPEAK OUT

"I was a human machine"
Aleksander Zielinski

MIND STALKERS

The *South China Morning Post* reported on Jan. 25 1995, that an assistant professor at the University of Science & Technology, Hong Kong, had filed a $100 million suit against the U.S. government for implanting mind-control devices in his teeth. Huang Si-ming charges that the devices were implanted during root canal work in 1991 while he was studying at the University of Iowa, according to the *Morning Post* reporter Patricia Young. Another student at the University of Iowa, who, like Huang, was born in China, had gone on a shooting spree, and the feds, Huang says, put the devices in his teeth to find out if he was involved.

The Hong Kong professor says he suffered an Alzheimer's disease-like memory loss that hampered his teaching. It stopped, he says, only when he sought legal aid to mount his lawsuit. Besides the U.S., the suit names the University of Science & Technology on the grounds that it was involved in continuing the mind control work. It also seeks punitive damages of $1 million from the defendants for "low ethical standards."

Huang claims that one of the devices in his teeth can read his thoughts and talk to his mind when he's asleep. A second device, he believes, transmits pictures of what he sees to a receiver for recording. The mind controller, he says, can drive him to "bad" behavior. Neither the university nor the U.S. Consulate in Hong Kong would comment on the suit, according to reporter Young.

At first glance this story might be dismissed as the ravings of a deranged individual. However, many of the supposedly outrageous claims made by Mr. Huang and others can be produced using technology developed specifically for mind control operations. Even the claims by Mr. Huang of some kind of implant being secretly placed in one of his teeth is known in the dark world of mind control victims. Writer Philip K. Dick speculated that he may have been implanted with a device after a trip to the dentist.

A "white paper" published in 1991 by the U.S. Global Strategy Council, a Washington-based organization, under the chairmanship of Ray Cline, former Deputy Director of the CIA, describes the foreign and domestic uses foreseen for laser weapons, isotropic radiators, infra-sound, non-nuclear electromagnetic pulse generators, and high-powered microwave emitters. All for the use of mind control.

MIND STALKERS

MARTTI KOSKI

A number of people have surfaced recently, all claiming to have been the victims of clandestine mind control experiments and harassment. In 1981, Ottawa resident Martti Koski wrote down his thoughts and feelings concerning his belief that he was being "attacked" mentally by mind control experiments.

"In the beginning I simply thought I was slowly going mad. I knew it wasn't normal to hear 'voices' and mine were with me for two to three hours every day. I felt they came at me through the ceiling from the suite above me. But, I wasn't really worried. I had resigned myself to the thought I was suffering from some sort of neurotic disorder, impossible to get rid of, but harmless enough.

"In the late summer of 1979, after four years of this 'talk,' things suddenly got a lot worse. I seemed to lose control of most of my normal body functions and emotions. It was as if someone or something could control my sleep, my sense of smell and taste. Finally, I couldn't even work. I'm a welder and I came to be unable to breathe in any air contaminated with carbon dioxide.

"By now 'the voices' were with me 24 hours a day. I was being talked to every waking hour. I was allowed minimal sleep - about an hour a day. My heartbeat became erratic and finally uncontrollable. In December 1979, I was admitted to the University of Alberta Hospital in Edmonton, the victim of a 'heart attack.' It was in the hospital I first suspected I was the victim of something more sinister than my body's own normal reaction to physical or emotional illness.

"For the first time the 'voice' identified itself. It told me it was a spokesman for the RCMP (Royal Canadian Mounted Police), and that I had been selected for 'training' as a spy. The first phase of my training would be to learn how to survive in a Russian insane asylum. The hospital would serve as my training ground.

"I remained in the hospital for three days, the subject of many bizarre and strange encounters and experiments. In one instance, I was given medication but simultaneously warned by 'the voice' not to take it as it was poisoned. When I did take it, I suffered heart palpitations.

MIND STALKERS

"When I left the hospital, I returned to my apartment. But, I again experienced problems with my breathing and extreme headaches. I decided to flee my home to seek release from the problems that were hounding me. I stayed away from my apartment for 10 days, living in cheap hotels--but I was not left alone. My sleep continued to be disrupted, I decided to look for help again at the hospital, but it was the same as the first time, it was still a 'spy school' where I was 'in training.'

"This time the 'training' involved stealing shirts and engaging in a kind of black market where cigarettes were used to buy services from other patients (inmates). As in my first experience, some of the doctors and some patients participated in the playacting to create the impression of a Russian insane asylum. One doctor I remember by name was Dr. Peter Hayes. I returned to my apartment, but one morning was awakened by a phone call from someone who hung up as soon as I answered. Immediately gas poured into my room for about 15 seconds causing my mouth to fill with blood. Then the voice told me this was my last warning.

"Afraid for both my sanity and my life I decided to return to my native Finland, a decision that was to convince me, more than ever, of the RCMP intrusion into and takeover of my life. I traveled to Toronto by Greyhound bus pursued all the while by 'the voices.' On this trip I noticed a marked RCMP car seemed to be following the bus for several hours. It was also on this bus trip that I got the first hint of the kind of experimentation I was being subjected to.

"The voices began to call me the 'Microwave Man,' and all the while the 'spy training' exercises continued. The voices told me that others like me were being trained all over the country and world to be unwitting spies and assassins. Unlike myself, others were not able to 'perceive' the voices in their heads. Instead the victims would go about their daily activities not realizing that they were being subliminally trained to perform when called upon. A frightening thought.

"Among other things, I was told what food to eat and what food was dangerous. If I ate forbidden food, I suffered severe heartburn and feverishness. The voices told me I needn't worry about my credit card spending as my line of credit had been extended to unlimited. I was given my first 'assignment' (to find out the population of Toronto and then how many men and how many women).

MIND STALKERS

"My voices became Finnish-speaking, female voices. Things in Finland were no better than they had been in Canada. The voices clung to me. The one change was they now identified themselves as being from the star Sirius.

"My return journey to Canada by ship, train and plane took over five days and nights, during which time I was not allowed to sleep at all. Back home in Edmonton the strange occurrences piled themselves one on another. I was subjected to several toxic gas experiments. It seemed to me now other tenants in the building were either agents of the RCMP or cooperating with the police force in their experiments.

"In an elaborate and excruciating experiment that involved hypnosis and supporting special effects employing fire trucks circling around me, I was presented with a program of indoctrination to convince me criticism of the American society was a 'cancer' and a threat to us all. I was told I was 'unclean' and 'contaminated' with this 'cancer.' The fire trucks were to be used in a massive cleansing or washing away of the contagion.

"By now it was early April. The days were warming up. I discovered the power of the microwaves were lessened in the open air. I was able to sleep out on the grass in the sunshine. This sleep, the first true sleep I had in months, was enough for me to begin to rebuild my will to resist the forces at work against me.

"As soon as I began to resist, the experimentation began to ease off. I still hear the Finnish voices, but the talk is less intensive. They call this stage 'custody.' My fear for my health and life continues, as well as my worries about what is in store for the entire Canadian society.

"I know my story sounds like the plot from some low budget science fiction spy thriller that could never happen in real life. The problem is it did happen in my life. And it could happen in yours if you don't join me in my battle today to expose and resist this attack on human dignity. If what has happened to me is any indication of what can be accomplished using some kind of 'mind control machinery,' then heaven help the common man. I was told by the voices that thousands of others like me have been trained. I fear for the future."

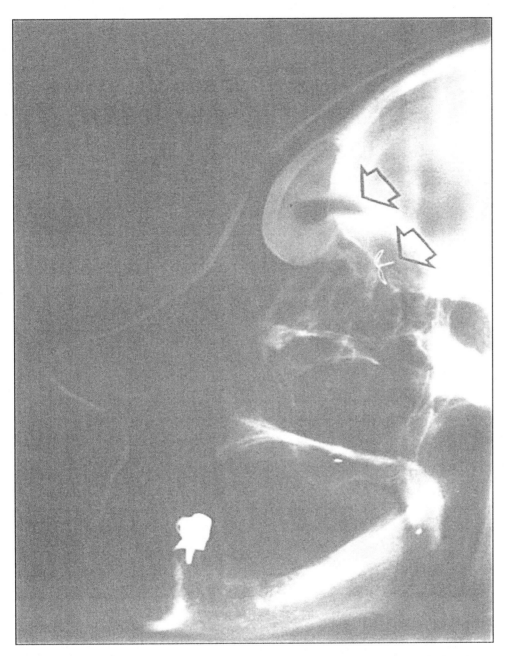

Despite their bizarre claims, some victims have offered proof of their experiences in the form of x-rays and MRIs that show unexplained metallic objects in their brains.

MIND STALKERS

MIKI TERRY

Miki Terry refers to herself and others who believe they are victims of electronic or microwave mind control harassment as "wavies." Terry thinks that her electronic stalkers are not secret government agents, but are "criminal types" who have bought their mind control devices from mail order companies. Terry believes these "mind stalkers" are harassing her and others simply for the fun of it.

"During the two years that I have been camped out at my mother's house trying to fight and survive the personal abuse that some locals have been directing at me with their electronic weaponry, I have become convinced that the perpetrators of the abuse are sick criminals who are being used as pawns in a war against America. Whether they realize that fact or not does not change the reality that they are participating in a war against America and they are fighting against America and against Americans and against themselves. If they win, they will die along with the largest percentage of the American population. There has been more and more evidence brought to my attention, cynical as my attention always is, that there really is a secret war going on among citizens of this country who are working to destroy it and themselves.

"In hearing the subliminal anti-Americanisms being broadcast over large areas, and in talking to other people who are being abused in very similar fashion, the pattern is becoming unmistakable. The people chosen to dish out the abuse are weak, self-hating, sick in mind and spirit and emotion, who get a kick out of hurting people. They are chosen to be jerked around with the easy handles of their obsessive sickness.

"They are led to escalate the electronic mind war to destroy America. What is going on is so sick and so hard to take to court because of the remote aspect of it that it is being kept more secret from the public and out of the hands of law enforcement than most abuse and weaponry in today's world. It is really happening to many people, and it can be proven in a way that evil cannot usually be proven if it involves mystery, sabotage, illusion, and hints of otherworldly involvement.

"I don't want to argue about MK-ULTRA propaganda from things that might have happened before I was born. I don't want to argue about the hints of sneaky goings on that are rumored all over the net. The web is full of sensation seekers.

MIND STALKERS

"I have also found that the electronic weapon users are using information gleaned from different sources, including the old Cold War research papers that have been promoted as though they were all true, when it is very obvious that some of it is disinformation to throw people off the real track.

"Some of the practices that have been used in Business Seminars and Sales Seminars as Neuro-Linguistic Programing, and some of the New Age/Alternative Religion research are forms of mind control, they employ ideas learned from cult groups on how to control their members. There remains the fact though that there are many people involved in an electronic war on Americans that is much bigger than most Americans are aware of. Really! Who is using the electronic weapons on random individuals to harass them in their own homes 24 hours a day? Would the Government subsidize punk perverts to harass and anonymously and remotely torture people with non-lethal weapons 24 hours a day? With no end result except eventual death and the silencing of mental horror.

"Actually, who would subsidize 24 hours a day surveillance and subliminal communications that are extremely confusing, with most of it involving reminding the victim that they are under surveillance? After talking to the other 'wavies' and various types of victims of e-weapons who are on-line and reading the information that is on-line, I am totally convinced that common criminals of the most sick kind are trying to be imitation 'controllers' of a mind control abuse sport. The supposed controllers and bullies are using electronics that can be obtained through mail order catalogs.

"They are devoting their lives to listening for footsteps and toilet flushes, watching surveillance cameras for changes in facial expressions and twitches of muscles. None of the 'controllers' has ever proposed a program or plan. They ceaselessly babble on about stupid perverted nonsense, and about what the victim is doing, as though they didn't already know what they are doing without having to be told. The government research about the e-weapons has been in the public, even if largely unnoticed, for a long time. While it is obvious from the research papers of the 1970s that there was some government involvement during the Cold War days of American history, the fact seems to be now that the weapons are in the hands of American street criminals and wanna-be-perverts. A big part of the confusion has been that the information about the e-weapons is from old government papers, but let's get current and realistic. It is obviously criminal perverts who are actively involved with e-weapons now."

Robert Naeslund

In 1991, Robert Naeslund detailed his mind control experiences brought about by an implant placed into his head during surgery. What make's Naeslund's story so compelling is the fact that in 1983 he was successful in convincing a surgeon to examine x-rays of his head. X-rays that clearly showed the presence of some kind of foreign object.

"Ever since an operation at Soder Hospital in Stockholm at the end of the 1960's, I have been used in a medical experiment which has meant a lot of suffering and been very painful. The operation was performed by Dr. Curt Strand, who inserted a foreign object, a so-called brain transmitter, in my head through the right nasal passage. For many years I have tried to get help from Swedish physicians and even from the National Board of Health and Welfare (Socialstyrelsen). However, I was confronted by doctors who became my enemies and I was, among other things, declared mentally ill and placed in a mental hospital.

"In 1983 I came in contact with Prof. P.A. Lindstrom at the University of California, San Diego in the United States, who examined my X-rays. Many Swedish doctors had given written opinions about these, and stated that the X-rays were completely normal, that there was no foreign object in my head. Prof. Lindstrom wrote in one of his many statements that in his opinion there was indeed a foreign object in my head, obviously placed there without my permission. After Prof. Lindstrom wrote his opinion, about ten other doctors in different countries have given written statements which attest to the implanted transmitters in my head. The statements clearly show that Swedish doctors, in collusion with Intelligence Operations, have given false reports concerning this case. Despite the substantial medical evidence which proves my case, I cannot get surgical help in Sweden to remove the many transmitters implanted in my head, which are active day and night, year after year."

MIND STALKERS

L.A. LINDSTROM, M.D.

July 27, 1983

Mr. R. Naeslund
Ervallakroken 27
12443 Bandhagen
SWEDEN
[not current address]

In response to your most recent letter regarding the roentgen films, I can only confirm that some foreign objects, most likely brain transmitters, have been implanted at the base of your frontal brain and in the skull.

The risk of such implantations is considerable and the risk of chronic infections and meningitis when the implantation has been made through the nose or the sinuses are real issues.

In my opinion, there is no excuse for such implantations if the patient has not been fully informed about the procedures, the purposes, the risks, the method of anesthesia, etc, and then gives a clear written consent.

I fully agree with Lincoln Lawrence, who in his book on page 27 wrote: "There are two particularly dreadful procedures which have been developed. E.D.O.M. – Radio-Hypnotic Intracerebral Control and Electronic Dissolution of Memory."

Many years go I had some discussions with Delgado. He asked me to apply my ultrasonic technique for his particular purpose of altering patient's behavior but I declined because we had entirely different aims and approaches. However, I found Delgado to be an intelligent but somewhat strange man.

Best wishes!

P.A. Lindstom, M.D.

MIND STALKERS

Cheryl Welsh

Cheryl Welsh feels that like herself, there are over one million people worldwide who have been victimized by mind control harassment. Welsh writes that the victims of mind control experiments are deliberately made to look mentally ill in order to cover-up the frightening truth.

"It is probable that classified computer-brain interface research has had a highly advanced technological leap similar to the pattern of the development of the atomic bomb weapon program. Many documented articles support this claim. It has been fifty years since the development of the atomic bomb and there have been major advancements in science, satellite technology, computers and information.

"In my case, mind control experimentation is the use of military electromagnetic frequency technology on human subjects in order to develop baseline studies of the brain, including brainwave studies and the study of personalities. As in radiation experiments, the lethal doses and the limits of technology are explored inhumanely.

"Mind control experiments are conducted as a result of development of behavior control weapons and are, like the radiation experiments, examples of science at its worst. Weapon testing programs are designed to disable and kill the enemy and therefore the experiments are also designed to destroy. There are over 500 documented cases of victims in the United States, one million alleged victims in Russia and cases in Germany, England, Canada, Finland, and South America.

"A few of the main similarities between victims are as follows. Women, prisoners and mental patients are a few of the powerless groups targeted in U.S. government experimentation. Most of the victims describe long term experimentation, some over 30 years. All ages, socioeconomic and political groups are represented in mind control experiments. This is a wide area of research and there are probably many umbrella projects to test many different parameters of behavior control weapons. Government experimentation with behavior control technology is based on psychological principles of war. For example, multiple personalities are thought to be caused by traumatic experiences. To learn how to control and destroy people, the experiments are designed to reliably create multiple personalities.

MIND STALKERS

"The U.S. government is using mental illness as a cover-up of mind control experimentation. Many of the experiments are designed to mimic mental illness. For example, the mental illness diagnosis manual for psychiatrists states that the mentally ill patient puts unusual meaning or interpretations into normal objects. The experimenters can engineer visual and audio patterns and change the amount and timing of any environment in a specific way to make the victim see what a mentally ill person would see. In my case, I have videotaped evidence of this effect. A report by a university statistics professor confirmed an extremely high amount of red and white cars on two separate occasions when compared with normal car color populations.

"With no meaningful evaluation, mental illness is the given explanation for the million plus victims. The concurrent development of technology, the U.S. government's history of involvement in mind control experiments and their motive to research this area can also strongly support the fact that these are victims of government experimentation. Further investigation of this situation is necessary rather than dismissing it as mental illness. I and most survivors have not been able to obtain help. This is typical in government cover up situations. And because of the nature of the technology itself, any efforts to stop the experimentation can be sabotaged with the mind control technology itself.

"I have gone to the police, lawyers, private investigators, newspapers, magazines, organizations such as the ACLU, government agencies such as the U.S. Attorney General, Congressman Glenn, Kennedy, Feinstein, Sharp and more. The answers vary from 'you are crazy,' 'you have to know the source of the experiment and have monitoring equipment evidence,' 'we don't handle cases such as this, it is out of our area of expertise,' to no reply, or 'we are aware of the situation but it will take years and over $100,000 to pursue in court,' and many other creative ways of saying no.

"Victims also cannot get around the unavailability of necessary government documents classified under the National Security Act. There is documented evidence that the superpowers have developed mind control weapons and that the use of these weapons is classified and controlled by the National Security Act. In the meantime, the government system is failing the mind control victim in the same way that it failed the radiation victim. I use what tools that I have, such as research of open literature and networking, a painfully slow process.

MIND STALKERS

"At this point, none of the victims, singly or as a group has the funds to stop the experimentation. I do not have the funds to rent or buy signal analyzers to document signals that the government would surely cover up or jam. Some victims have documented some unusual signals, but it is such a small piece of evidence and is not directly tied to the government source. The evidence has been ignored or discounted.

"I am currently organizing a group of victims to be monitored by experts. Experts are necessary to verify information for court cases and Congressional hearings. Video-tape evidence and other mind control experimentation evidence does not directly tie the U.S. government to my allegation and therefore is not accepted by courts, congressional hearings, or UN complaints. There are many other basic and complicated reasons for the government system and its failure to help victims in any significant way. The system obviously needs to be changed."

Philip K. Dick

Perhaps the best-known victim of alleged mental harassment was the late writer, Philip K. Dick. A series of strange, life altering occurrences began to inundate the author's life. According to Dick, he received "microwave boosted telepathic transmissions," as he called them, that started on March 20, 1974. He became aware of this after he was struck in the forehead with what he perceived as a pink colored laser beam. After that experience he was showered with endless streams of visual and audio data. Initially, this overpowering onslaught of mental messages was extremely unpleasant, he termed them as, "die messages."

Within the following week he reported being kept awake by "violet phosphene activity, eight hour's uninterrupted." A description of this event in a fictionalized version appears in Dick's brilliant series of novels the *VALIS Trilogy*.

The content of this phosphene activity was in the form of modern abstract graphics followed by Soviet Music serenading his head. Dick supposed that a radical drop in GABA fluid might have accounted for these strange voices and images. However, after awhile, Dick began to believe that he was being harassed by a Soviet Psychotronic transmission being directed at him from a satellite high overhead.

MIND STALKERS

Another possibility exists that Philip K. Dick might have received a brain implant during dental surgery which occurred just prior to his fabled first visit from **VALIS** (Vast Active Living Intelligence System) chronicled in his books, *Radio Free Albemuth*, and *VALIS*.

In March 1974, Phil went to have some major work done on his teeth. Later, when he arrived back home, a pain killer was delivered from the local pharmacy. The delivery person was a young woman who had a Christian Fish charm hanging from her neck. The young lady said a few cryptic words then left. Phil theorized that this young lady, who claimed to be a Christian, delivered to him some sort of veiled gnostic knowledge, which proceeded to unfold its answers gradually to a whole host of hidden metaphysical secrets for several years afterwards.

Another scenario might have been that this young lady was on an intelligence mission, delivering some kind of drug to not only soothe Phil's painful mouth, but that would also help activate the hidden devices secretly inserted into his head during the dental surgery. Another possible explanation is that the short cryptic sentence The Fish Lady uttered was in reality some sort of codeword which triggered this mind control apparatus into operation. Oddly enough, it was later, on this very same day, that Phil's "visions" first appeared.

To suggest that a dentist might have planted Psychotronic receptors into the mouth and head of Philip K. Dick might seem utterly ridiculous. However, rumors that certain dentists have participated in mind control operations using dental implants have some basis in fact. The opportunity to insert such devices during dental surgery, while the patient is anesthetized, can be easily accomplished.

According to conspiratologist John Judge, Uri Geller's dentist was the person who first developed some of the earliest mind control devices. These devices were radio transmitters that could be implanted into the jaw and teeth so that instructions could be heard through the teeth.

In the beginning, Phil felt the emanations invading his mind were of a malevolent nature. However, in time, he began to believe they were something entirely different. In a letter dated February 10, 1978, Phil went into depth on these Psychotronic transmissions, claiming that they "seemed sentient." Phil felt that an alien life form existing in the upper layer of the Earth's atmosphere had been attracted by the Soviet Psychotronic transmissions.

Apparently, this alien life form operated as a "station," tapping into an interplanetary communication grid that, "contained and transmitted vast amounts of information." Initially, what Phil received were the Soviet transmissions, but eventually this alien life form, whom Phil called **Zebra** (and later, **VALIS**) became "attracted or potentiated by the Soviet microwave Psychotronic transmissions." Instead of Soviet mind control signals from a satellite, Dick became convinced that **VALIS** was communicating with him by direct transmissions into his brain.

Over the years that followed, this alien entity, according to Dick, vastly improved his mental and physical well being in a number of ways. It (**Zebra**) gave Phil "complex and accurate information about myself and also about my infant son, which, Zebra said, had a critical and undiagnosed birth defect which required emergency and immediate surgery. My wife rushed our baby to the doctor and told the doctor what I had said (more precisely what **Zebra** had said to me) and the doctor discovered that it was true. Surgery was scheduled for the following day. Our son would have died otherwise." (Phil's wife Tessa, and others have since confirmed this story regarding the medical conditions of himself and son, Christopher.)

Phil felt **Zebra** was totally benign, and it held great contempt for the Soviets and their Psychotronic experiments. Furthermore, **Zebra** informed Phil that the Earth was dying, and that spray cans were "destroying the layer of atmosphere in which **Zebra** existed." Some have questioned whether in fact Phil had created an immense hoax, or if he was, actually, "crazy as a soapdish," as Harlan Ellison stated in an interview with Larry King. Were his "visions" simply delusions, which Phil tried to make some sense of? Or could it all have been exactly as Phil first assumed: Psychotronic mind control transmissions beamed at him from Russia, or from somewhere else.

CHAPTER NINE

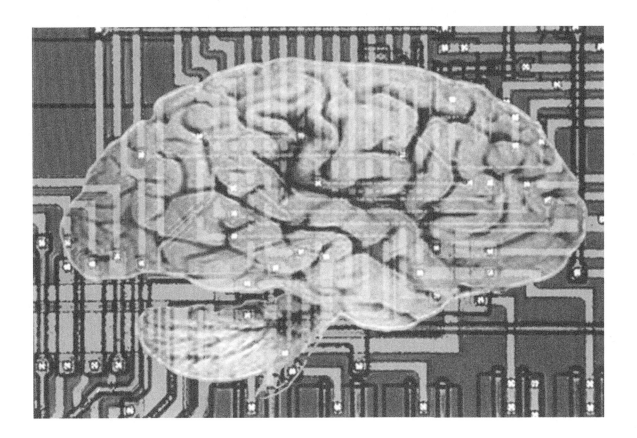

HARASSMENT OF VICTIMS

MIND STALKERS

**The same people who can deny others everything
are famous for refusing themselves nothing.**

Leigh Hunt

MIND STALKERS

According to Julianne McKinney, Director of the now defunct Electronic Surveillance Project, mind control and human behavior modification can present itself in many forms. One method used to seemingly "ready" a victim is overt harassment. This method is apparently also used as a weapon against "whistle blowers" or others who get in the way.

Overt Harassment may be intended to "precondition" individuals for eventual long-term electronic harassment. Persons terrified by unexplained overt harassment are not likely to cope with the sudden onset of electronic harassment in any more reasoned fashion. The fact that the overt harassment continues in these cases even after the electronic targeting commences suggest that the objective is to maintain long-term extremes of stress.

Many of the overt harassment tactics investigated are surfacing in cases which have no apparent forms of electronic harassment. These are cases involving so-called "whistle blowers" who, because of their inside knowledge of certain potentially newsworthy events, pose particular threats of embarrassment to the Government or to government-affiliated employers. Research has shown that electronic harassment is beginning to surface as a form of retaliation against persons who try to help electronic "harassees." Individuals who have experienced overt forms of harassment all describe a frightening similar scenario.

- Sudden, bizarrely-rude treatment, isolation and acts of harassment

  and vandalism by formerly friendly neighbors.

- Harassing telephone calls, which continue even after the targeted individual obtains new, unlisted telephone numbers.

- Mail interception, theft, tampering and noise campaigns.

MIND STALKERS

While unrelenting harassing telephone calls might be considered in this context, other tactics are employed. Blaring horns, whistles, sirens, garbage disposal (run concurrently in apartment settings, for excessively prolonged periods of time), and amplified transmissions of recorded "general racket" have been used on a recurrent basis under circumstances intended to persuade the individual that he or she is under surveillance.

In all of these cases, the individuals' neighbors apparently pretend to be oblivious and/or indifferent to these sudden, continuous explosions of noise. Door slamming is also a popular pastime, particularly in apartment buildings.

One individual reported that, during a peak period of harassment, the neighbor across the hall began entering and leaving his apartment every ten minutes, slamming his door loudly on each occasion. This was a daily occurrence, encompassing periods of several hours, over a period of several months. This apparently served to trigger a door-slamming "chain reaction" on the part of neighbors both on that floor and on the floors immediately above and below. When the neighbor was politely asked to close his door more quietly, he slammed the door in her face. Prior to commencement of this harassment, the neighbor had apparently been quite friendly and courteous.

In another case, the primary door-slammer was an employee of Radix Systems, Inc., Rockville, MD, a DoD contractor engaged in the "super-secret" research and development of some type of electronic equipment. Several individuals reported recurrent, loud, strange noises in their ventilation systems during the preliminary stages of their harassment. One individual complained of being recurrently awakened in the middle of the night by the sound of wires being fed into his (independent) ventilation system. On checking further, he found that a tubular construction had been built into his vent system which appears to lead to the apartment upstairs. His upstairs neighbor is employed by the Department of Justice.

A number of individuals report that occupants of upstairs and downstairs apartments appear to follow them from room to room, tapping on the floor or engaging in other activities which appear intended to advertise an ongoing surveillance. The Justice Department employee mentioned before, went as far as to offer an apology to her neighbor for an all-night "pacing" in her bedroom. She claimed to be an insomniac.

MIND STALKERS

The pacing-about continued during her recent 36-hour absence from the area. When her contact politely alerted her to the fact that her apartment had apparently been entered during her absence, she told him to mind his own business and then immediately complained to the building manager that he was stalking her. She conveniently forgot to inform the building manager that she had been stealing his newspapers on a regular basis. On one occasion, she handed him a week's accumulation of those papers, claiming that they had been left outside the door of another apartment. Her reason for collecting and saving the newspapers which had not been delivered to her directly is unknown.

Recurrent confrontations by unusually hostile strangers and comments by strangers which appear intended to evoke "paranoid" reactions. In this context, several people have reported confrontations with "homeless" people who, on closer examination, were found to be fastidiously clean, though garbed in offbeat fashion (wigs included).

Entries into the individual's residence, during late-night hours while he or she is sleeping, or during the day when the individual is elsewhere. In virtually all such cases, the burglars leave evidence of their visits, such as moving objects, or by committing petty and not-so-petty acts of vandalism. In two cases, the burglar's "calling card" was to slaughter caged pets, leaving the mangled carcasses inside their locked cages. In one case, the burglar stole several pieces of correspondence and left a packet of crack cocaine behind as a "calling card."

In another case, a harassed woman reported that a tremendous amount of money had been stolen from a hiding place in her apartment, within hours after she had withdrawn the money from her bank. There were no signs of entry into her apartment. The police conducted a cursory inquiry which failed to produce evidence of a crime worthy of investigation. (This case is an anomaly. Money is usually not stolen. Documents and other papers appear to be the preferred objects when theft does occur). In two cases, massive rectal bleeding accompanied the sudden onset of severe gastrointestinal disturbances. One of these individuals abruptly terminated the process simply by changing the locks on her door. Sleep disruption is often a favorite of the unknown harrassers. This is usually achieved by means of overt and electronic harassment. Sleep deprivation, as a tactic, invariably surfaces when the targeted individual begins exhibiting a strong emotional and irrational response to the other forms of harassment.

Vehicles invite peculiarly ferocious attacks in these harassment campaigns, slashed tires, smashed windows, oil drainage, oil contamination, destruction of electronic components and batteries. Harassment while driving is often reported. One individual, for example, was tailgated at a high rate of speed by two vehicles, while concurrently being threatened with a gun by one of the vehicles' occupants.

Two others narrowly avoided what happened to be deliberately attempted collisions by drivers who quickly sped away from the scene. One avoided three attempts in four days at being run off the road. One survived after being run off the road in two incidents within a one-week period, which resulted in "totaling" of her two vehicles. Another narrowly avoided being crushed into an expressway retaining wall, on four occasions, by an off-duty metro bus, as well as, within the same time frame, being "fried" by two suddenly malfunctioning household appliances which afterwards repaired themselves.

It should be noted that, in some of these cases, "accidental" deaths do occur. A freelance researcher reported that his mother drove off a cliff to her death, during a period when he was researching evidence that a high level State Department official had passed A-bomb secrets to the Soviet Government during WWII.

The accident occurred shortly after her car had undergone routine maintenance. She was returning from a dental appointment when the accident occurred. Witnesses state that it appeared that she had suddenly stepped on the accelerator before running off the road. The accident served to terminate this person's research project.

There is also the recent death of a woman in Lexington, MO, who was killed when the brakes on her tractor failed. Prior to her death, the woman had been collecting affidavits from people who believe they are the targets of government harassment and experimentation when her "accident" occurred. Suicides and murder might also qualify as "staged accidents," particularly where "plausibly deniable" government involvement has surfaced.

MIND STALKERS

One person, (driven to extremes of stress by ongoing electronic harassment focusing on her children) killed her child in an effort to protect her from further pain. It appears that lasers were being used in this individual's case. The targeting intensified after she called the Soviet Embassy to report the harassment, which she believed to be U.S. Government-sponsored. It became even more deadly when, in a further show of defiance, she then called the representative of the Iraqi Government to portray the U.S. Government's war in the Middle East as "hypocritical." She is now hospitalized in a Midwestern facility, where the experimentation is continuing.

Another woman, during a telephone conversation, was told by an employee of a local power company that, if she valued the lives of her children, she would drop her public opposition to the company's installation of high power lines. Since receiving that threat, the individual's 11-year-old daughter has been reduced to extremes of pain, resulting in her recurrent hospitalization for treatment of illnesses which cannot be diagnosed. It is also apparent to this woman that her three-year-old son is on the receiving end of externally-induced auditory input.

People who have tried to resolve their respective situations by trying to work through the "proper establishment" channels such as the police, FBI, local, state and federal court systems, or even trying to contact their respective political representatives in Washington, D.C., have invariably encountered the following:

1. Apathy, indifference and/or professed helplessness on the part of members of congress and state legislators.

2. Dismissal and/or attempted discrediting by psychiatrists who refuse to include the terms, "government harassment," "mind-control experimentation" and "torture" in their vocabulary.

Several individuals, thinking that psychiatrists might help to alleviate the stress associated with their harassment, received treatments which clearly pointed to cooperation between their psychiatrists and members of the U.S. Intelligence community. One such psychiatrist, in fact, bragged about being a member of the U.S. Intelligence "inner circle," informing his patient that her harassment was a "Pavlovian Experiment," intended to "break her."

MIND STALKERS

The Air Loom

Although our modern electronic age has been in existence only since the turn of this century, individuals have claimed that their minds were being remotely influenced and controlled by people and machines for at least two centuries. The medical world has classified people reporting these experiences as delusional. The most common diagnosis was what is now termed Paranoid Schizophrenia.

The first recorded case of paranoia in medical literature was James Tilly Matthews, a London tea-broker who claimed his mind was being controlled by a gang operating a machine he called an "Air Loom." It was supposedly hidden in a London cellar and sent out invisible, magnetic rays.

Matthews believed machines like the Air Loom were also controlling the minds of members of the British Parliament. He wrote letters to its members warning them about the machines and the conspiracy behind it. Matthews was committed to Bethlem Hospital for being insane. His case was published in 1810 by John Haslam.

The idea of projecting thoughts and ideas at a distance, so often reported in modern cases of alleged mind control, is also reflected in James Matthews' descriptions of his torment, listed here by John Haslam, then in charge of Bethlem Hospital.

"The Air Loom machine which assails Matthews, works on a variety of fuels of a disgusting nature, including 'effluvia of dogs – stinking human breath – putrid effluvia – stench of the cesspool,' and so forth. Its rays assault both the body and mind, producing a list of calamities hitherto unheard of and for which no remedy has been yet discovered. These include: 'Fluid Locking,' which renders Matthews speechless; 'Cutting Soul from Sense,' which causes his feelings to be severed from his thoughts; 'Stone-making,' which creates bladder stones; 'Thigh-talking,' which produces the auditory distortion of one's ear being in one's thigh; 'Kiteing,' or the capacity to hijack the brain and to implant thoughts in it beyond the control and resistance of the sufferer; 'Sudden death-squeezing' or 'Lobster-cracking,' which involve the deployment of a magnetic field to stop the circulation and impede the vital motions; 'Stomach-skinning,' which removes the skin from the belly; 'Apoplexy-working with the nutmeg grater,' which violently forces fluids into the head, often with lethal effects; 'Lengthening the brain,' or in other words, forcible thought distortion, which can 'cause good sense to appear as insanity, and convert truth to libel;' 'Thought-making,' which is the extraction by suction of one train of thought and its replacement with another."

Matthews produced keyed diagrams of the Air Loom showing the different levers that bring about the various tortures by producing modulations of the magnetic waves and the members of the gang which operated it. Although his family and many members of the community testified that he was a threat to no one, Matthews eventually died in 1815 while still an inmate of Bethlem.

Was Matthews simply insane or was there some actual connection to a form of mind control from an outside source? This is the same question being faced today by people who insist that they are victims of mind control by high-technology devices.

Unlike Matthews, modern victims of supposed mental harassment can point to any number of declassified military and intelligence documents detailing the developing of technologies and methods with the same capabilities of mental control that some have described for years. These technologies involve elements of psychology, hypnosis, political conspiracies, and even devices that emit "rays" to control the behavior of others without their knowledge or consent.

The probability does exist that there could be a system in place that uses modern methods of electronics, microwaves and radio frequency, advanced hypnotism and drug therapy, in order to influence the minds of individuals or even groups. These techniques have been developed in order to take advantage of "known" human psychosis and other mental illnesses.

Canadian Psychiatrist, Dr. Colin Ross, has acknowledged that mind control techniques have been disguised as mental illness with the help of leading mental health professionals.

"Virtually every leading psychiatrist in North America between the 1940's and the 1970's was involved in some aspect of the CIA's mind control research."

CHAPTER TEN

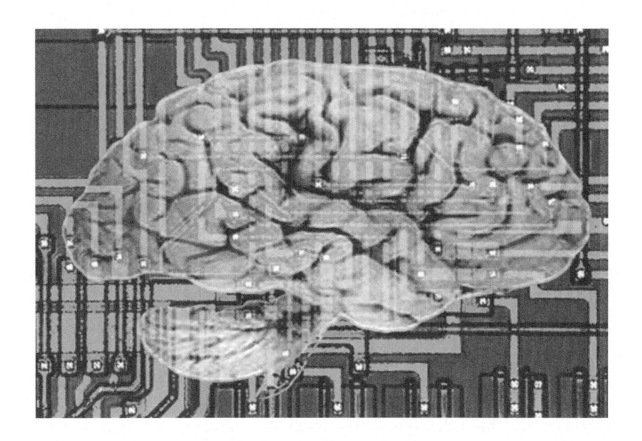

MIND CONTROL - IS IT TECHNICALLY FEASIBLE?

MIND STALKERS

The age of innocent faith in science and technology may be over.
Every major advance in the technological competence of man
has enforced revolutionary changes in the economic and
political structure of society.

Barry Commoner

MIND STALKERS

In Himeji Japan, a new remote-control system that uses brain waves has been developed that the inventor says could be a boon for the paralyzed. Hidenori Onishi has invented a device that senses brain-wave patterns and converts them into signals used to operate electrical appliances. He claims that the machine is the world's first brain-wave remote control aimed at a broad consumer market.

"We're already marketing remote-control products that are activated by touch, voice or breathing," said Onishi, whose Technos Japan Co. jointly developed the device with the Himeji Institute of Technology. "When your limbs are paralyzed and you can't use your voice, what you have left is your brain." Naoki Yoshida, a researcher at the College of Medical Technology at Hokkaido University, said the system could be useful to the handicapped, "if the system really responds to brain waves and it doesn't require training." He cautioned, however, that creating a system that responds to brain waves "seems very difficult."

The device in Onishi's lab looks like a pair of ski goggles. The goggles contain electrodes which are attached to a laptop-sized computer. It is called the Mind Control Tool Operating System, or MCTOS. The device will sell for just under five thousand dollars. Onishi says similar devices have been built, but remain either experimental or highly impractical. One device made in the United States requires that an electrode be implanted in the user's scalp, he said.

"The system requires no training by the user, because the brain waves the machine responds to are emitted simply by exercising the will," Onishi said. In practical terms, exercising the will means saying something like "Yes!" or "On!" inside your head.

Any strong mental affirmation sends out a brain signal that the electrodes apparently intercept and feed to the computer. The computer then activates the appropriate appliance. Nerve cells in the brain are constantly emitting a variety of electrical impulses, each of which has a distinctive wavelike pattern when monitored by an instrument called the electroencephalograph. MCTOS responds to a single type of brain impulse, the beta wave, which is produced in states of mental excitement. It can also be set up to operate by the electrical impulses emitted by rapid eye movement.

MIND STALKERS

"Brain waves are emitted by everyone," Onishi said. "But there are some types that are difficult to control and others that can be controlled quite easily." To prove his point, Onishi put on the electrodes, clenched his fists and closed his eyes. Electric bells started ringing on command and the TV responded to his every wish.

Items on the display menu, which looks like a computer screen and can be placed conveniently in front of the user, include television, stereo and electric bed control. A brain wave pulse turns the computer on, and more pulses are used to step through a menu of appliances and the desired actions by them. An Associated Press reporter who tested the system easily mastered simple tasks like turning on lights. More demanding activities such as changing television channels took a bit of extra thought, however.

Portable Mind Control Machines

Devices like the Mind Control Tool Operating System demonstrates that the technology for mind control does actually exist, and is most likely currently operational. Victims of mind control abuse have reported sighting electronic equipment that they think might be used in their harassment. One woman saw electronic equipment concealed inside a false-front upright piano being moved out of her apartment building. Another victim, while standing outside her house, noticed that a gray-colored, elongated boxlike device was being aimed at her bedroom from the window of a neighbor. A large, black-framed lens protruded from the end facing her window. The equipment was being operated by a stranger in a three-piece suit, who appeared to be quite startled to find that he was being observed.

It has been reported that portable electronic mind control emitters are being concealed in oversized, extremely heavy, sometimes expandable "briefcases" for use in public. Mobile emitters may be installed in cars or vans, possibly for the eventual use in civil disturbances.

Kai Bashir, author of the book *Mind Control Within the United States*, writes about her strange encounters with cars that she believes were carrying mind control machines targeting her and her family. "One afternoon while driving with my two daughters, a car overtook me. It moved fast. Yet the bumper sticker on it stuck. It read, **Watch that Child**. At that moment, my daughter Raki let out a piercing cry. The crying came in loud gasps. 'My body hurts, my body hurts,' she cried. Her cries became more shrill, 'My legs hurt.' After some time the cries quieted down.

"I searched for a clue to point in a direction where I found others who were zapped or experienced similar things. During the search, I went to a shop that sold jewelry and crystals. A lady who stood in the store told the owner knew of people that had experienced signs of mind control experimentation. Then she reached over and said, 'You know, they ride in cars carrying equipment, they follow a person around in a car and zap them.' 'What purpose does that serve?' I asked. 'Well,' she said, 'they have to try out new equipment on someone and since there are no volunteers, they use unwitting humans.'"

Black Helicopters

Black helicopters have for a number of years been attributed to such groups as secret UN troops to disguised UFOs. However, the bizarre story of Rex Niles and his sister may show that some black helicopters could be involved in electronic mind control harassment.

Rex Niles was the owner of a Woodland Hills California defense subcontracting firm. Recently, Niles was indicted by authorities investigating defense industry kickbacks. He became an extraordinarily cooperative witness in the investigation, until he was targeted by his enemies, who allegedly used Psychoelectronics as harassment. The following excerpt from the *Los Angeles Times* article on Niles is particularly interesting:

"He [Niles] produced testimony from his sister, a Simi Valley woman who swears that black helicopters have repeatedly circled her home. An engineer measured 250 watts of microwaves in the atmosphere outside Niles' house and found a radioactive disk underneath the dash of his car. A former high school friend, Lyn Silverman, claimed that her home computer went haywire when Niles stepped close to it."

MIND STALKERS

The behavior of Lyn Silverman's computer seems to suggest that Niles was being constantly bombarded by high-energy beams, probably microwaves. These beams could be keeping Niles in a constant state of cooperative behavior with the authorities. It has been shown in past experiments that microwaves can leave an individual confused and easily manipulated by outside influences.

What Is Known

Julianne McKinney in her publication titled: *Microwave Harassment and Mind Control Experimentation,* documents the experiences of people who reported harassment with what they claim are directed energy weapons. With the information that McKinney and other researchers have uncovered concerning mind control operations, these conclusions can be considered:

- The technology exists for the types of harassment.
  And experimentation reported by the victims.

- Hundreds of people worldwide have reported continuing
  experiments with effects which directed-energy weapons
  are designed to produce.

- U.S. government-sponsored research into the bioeffects of
  exposure to microwave radiation is extensive and continuing.

- The U.S. government has a past record of having engaged in
  mind-control experimentation; and various agencies of the
  government has a record of avoiding legal restrictions
  upon their activities.

- Neither Congress nor the courts appear willing to look closely
  into secret intelligence and weapons procurement programs.

- A number of U.S. Government agencies might have interest in
  testing directed-energy technologies on U.S. citizens under

non-clinical/non-controlled circumstances, DoD, to test ranges and degrees of "non-lethality;" DoE, to explore "safety" limits; CIA, to test "mind-control" capabilities, and NSA, for technological refinement.

■ There is an ongoing mind control project currently operating for reasons that are still not known. The project could be directed by official intelligence organizations, or could be the result of "rouge" groups operating independently of government/military sponsors.

E-Weapons And Their Victims

Eleanor White, an alleged victim of mental harassment, lists E-weapons victims as four basic types:

1. Guinea pigs

2. Corporate whistle blowers and workers' comp. claimants whose claims expose corporate misdeeds

3. Pleasure objects for surveillance and e-weapon holders who are sexual perverts

4. Unlucky individuals who inadvertently ended up at the wrong place at the wrong time and chosen apparently at random.

White believes that today's e-weapon guinea pigs are fundamentally different from the old-style institutional and child-abused MKULTRA victims in that the torturers never need to come face to face with their victims. Tracking and telemetry has reached science fiction levels of efficiency.

"So today's e-weapons victims zap and torture you thru the walls and floors, with silent weapons which can cause enough pain to force suicide and still leave not a single physical trace. The weapons don't even budge my very ferrous sheet steel cocoon, even while the spooks move objects within the enclosure."

MIND STALKERS

White says that today's E-weapons fall into two main classes:

1. Old-fashioned pulsed microwave (radar-like) weapons which can transmit voices into your skull (no receiver or implant required) and do other things like bathe you in a perpetual itch which causes you to scratch down to the point of bleeding without relief, and cause the sensation of hot needles in any body part, with genitalia preferred. Some victims are subjected to simple brute force maser burning of their skin.

2. New-fashioned weapons which use signal types that are probably unknown to unclassified science. These include the precise thru-the-wall and thru-sheet-steel CAT scanning equipment and most strikingly the remote manipulation equipment. I would also class the ability to energize unplugged appliances and to interrupt current in an AC line cord without actuating any switches as in this "second generation" class of e-weapons.

An Insiders View

The following is an interview with a CIA employee, who for obvious reasons, must remain anonymous. This interview was published in *Leading Edge* magazine, and we are pleased to be able to present this insider's view of what is going on behind the scenes.

Q: A career officer doesn't need to be debriefed by mind control does he?

A: You want to bet? This debriefing is done in such a way, in many causes, to cause actual memory damage.

Q: What you are suggesting, I guess, is that there is an invisible coup d'etat which has occurred in the United States?

A: There is a group of about eighteen or twenty people running this country. They have not been elected. The elected people are only figureheads for these guys who have a lot more power then even the President.

MIND STALKERS

Q: You mean the President is powerless?

A: Not exactly powerless. He has the power to make decisions on what is presented to him. The intelligence agencies tell him only what they want to tell him. Think of the Pentagon Papers. It is public knowledge that the CIA has falsified documents and done a host of other things. You have to wonder at American stupidity. What people don't know is that the global corporations have their own version of the CIA. They don't interface with the CIA, they have their own organizations, all CIA-trained. They also have double agents inside the CIA who are loyal to those corporations.

Q: What do you know about the use of pain-drug hypnosis?

A: They use several different things. I've seen guys coming back with blanks only in certain places of their memory. They use hypnosis and hypnosis, they'll be using at the same time a set of earphones which repeat: "You do not know this or that" over and over. They turn on the sonics at the same time, and the electrical patterns which give you memory are scrambled. You can't hear the ultrasonics and you can't feel it, unless they leave it on and then it boils your grey matter.

Q: I thought that research had stopped on ultrasonics?

A: Yeah, the research has stopped. They've gone operational. It ain't research any more. They know how to do it. Our Constitution doesn't permit us to do much that is legal.

Q: Do the police use mind control?

A: At the highest levels, yes. The FBI uses it, and they give a lot of help to local police. Let me tell you something, the cheapest commodity in the world is human beings. All you hear about are left-wing conspiracies to overthrow our government. You never hear about the right-wing conspiracies. Well, some of these right-wing groups are far more dangerous that the left-wing groups. The right wing is usually retired military. If the right-wing took over right now there would be a military dictatorship. We've go one right now, but it ain't overt, it's subtle.

MIND STALKERS

Q: You mean those twenty men you were talking about?

A: Yeah, if the people of this country actually knew that, they would say "NO" the next time they were asked to go to Vietnam or Iraq. We need the people behind us to fight a war, and if they knew the true facts, who's running things, there wouldn't be the following we'd need to defend the country. That fact alone keeps the sham of politics and free elections going. The American people, like most people, have to feel that they have some right in what they do, that they're the good guys. This is the reason we have never lost a war and have never won the peace. You've got to maintain the sham of freedom, no matter what. It wouldn't make any difference what party is in charge or whether it was the elected government or what is called the cryptocracy [or the Secret Government] that was running it; from an operational sense, the government would operate as it presently is.

Who Is In Control?

In his book, *Psychiatry and the CIA: Victims of Mind Control*, Dr. Harvey Weinstein quotes the following passage from a book entitled, *A battle for the Mind: A Physiology in Conversion and Brainwashing*, by William Sergeant (Greenwood Press, Westport, CT, 1957):

"By increasing the prolonged stress in various ways, or inducing physical debilitation, a more thorough alteration of the person's thinking process may be achieved. If the stress or physical debilitation, or both, are carried one stage further, it may happen that patterns of thought and behavior, especially those of recent acquisition, become disrupted.

"New patterns can then be substituted, or suppressed patterns allowed to reassert themselves; or the subject might begin to think or act in ways precisely contradicting his former ones. If a complete collapse can be produced by prolonging or intensifying emotional stress, the cortical slate may be wiped clean temporarily of its more recently implanted patterns of behavior, perhaps allowing other types of behavior to be substituted more easily. These new patterns can be reinforced to produce a more permanent effect on behavior if this is desired."

MIND STALKERS

The reasons that some people are being subjected to mind control operations can range from being a suspected political dissident, to having access to knowledge that is considered dangerous, either by government or corporate officials. The long-term objectives of these mind control harassment and experimentation campaigns appear to be trying to induce a sense of perverted "loyalty" toward the very agencies engaged in the individual's harassment. To confuse his or her priorities where the possibility of obtaining legal help might be concerned.

Those responsible for the harassment could also be trying to redirect the targeted individual's feelings of hopelessness, anger and frustration toward racial and ethnic groups. This would include hostility toward select political figures, such as the President of the United States, forcing the individual to commit an act of violence, whether suicide or murder, under conditions which he can be plausibly denied by the government.

Skeptics of mind control harassment have often countered that government agencies do not have the budget or capabilities to harass the great number of reported victims. However, some reports such as the Miki Terry case seem to suggest that mind control equipment can be easily obtained by non-government agencies and even criminals.

One victim reported her "voices" informed her that the technologies being used against her were stolen from the CIA by a maverick employee, who has copied the technology and sold it to criminals, stalkers and anyone else with enough money.

She reported this to the local FBI office and was allegedly informed by the agent that she would be awarded millions of dollars if she can produce the equipment and any of the personnel involved in her harassment. There is also the possibility that unethical psychiatrists and physicians either are involved in experiments of their own, or are being directed by corporate, government or criminal elements.

From military officers to prison inmates, the ranks of ordinary Americans who claim to have been the unwilling subjects of mind control research continue to grow. With the help of the Internet, many victims now have forums to express their frustrations, talk with others who have had similar experiences and possibly seek help from the unrelenting mental abuse.

MIND STALKERS

In the past, many alleged victims of mind control harassment felt that they were alone because of the belief that they were suffering strictly from mental illness. Now, victims are able to communicate with others who have also had the same experiences and frustrations with being ignored by doctors and law enforcement agencies.

These communications are now finally convincing investigators that something more than mental illness is happening to these unfortunate people. However, some researchers are now reporting that they themselves are being targeted by mind control harassment. Leading some to drop out from further investigation for fear of their own sanity.

Unfortunately, until the time comes when someone will be caught red-handed with a mind control device, the stigma of mental illness will continue to plague the victims of mind control abuse. Hopefully that day will come before the use of such devices
becomes so widespread that the citizens of this planet will be forever unable to free themselves from the mind stalkers.

•   •   •

If you have any questions or comments you can now e-mail Commander X at:

commanderx12@hotmail.com

Or, you can always send a letter to:
**Commander X
C/O Global Communications
P.O. Box 753
New Brunswick, NJ 08903**

www.conspiracyjournal.com

MIND STALKERS

Index Of Secret Mind Control Projects

ARTICHOKE: Project Bluebird, renamed in August 1951 at urging of CIA's Allen Dulles. First instance of LSD testing on involuntary human subject resulting in death. First operational use, 1954, on "Communist Bloc individuals."

BLUEBIRD: Commenced in 1949 under CIA auspices by Office of Scientific Intelligence (OSI) to develop "unconventional warfare techniques, including behavioral drugs." Domestic human testing involved.

CHATTER: US Navy program started in 1947 aimed at weakening "if not eliminating free will in others" via psychological and pharmacological "terminal" operations with the CIA. Tested in 1952 on unwitting foreign subjects. Code-named: CASTIGATE.

MK-DELTA: Started in 1960 by the CIA, the purpose was to determine how to program behavior and attitudes in the general population using Fine-tuned electromagnetic subliminal programming operating on VHF, UHF and HF. Also known as: DEEP SLEEP.

MK-SEARCH: Follow on project from MKULTRA, which was officially said to be "terminated" following Freedom of Information Act searches exposure of human experimentation. Project MKSEARCH started in 1966 through 1972.

MK-ULTRA: Started on April 3, 1953 as umbrella CIA project for "special research purposes." The program considered "various means for controlling human behavior of which drugs were only one aspect. Others being: radiation, electro-shock, psychology, psychiatry, sociology, anthropology, harassment substances, and paramilitary devices and materials." Clandestine experiments conducted on "involuntary human subjects."

MOONSTRUCK: Research and development by the CIA of electronic implants in the brain and teeth. Implanted during surgery or surreptitiously during abduction, the implants could be used for tracking, mind and behavior control and covert operations. This was achieved through electronic stimulation of the brain (ESB).

MIND STALKERS

ORION: Developed by the Air Force in 1958, this project used drugs, hypnosis, and ESB using Radar and microwaves modulated at ELF frequencies. Created for top security personnel debriefing, mental programming and to insure security and loyalty.

PANDORA: A program to monitor Soviet microwave bombardment of the US embassy in Moscow, known as the "war on Tchaikowsky Street," during the sixties and seventies. Developed under the auspices of the Defense Advanced Research Projects Agency (DARPA). Project personnel believed to have permitted continued Soviet radiation bombardment to observe prolonged effects on US embassy staff. Project used as a "cover" for ongoing EM mind control research and development using radio frequency (RF) and direct "neural manipulation by remote radar."

PIQUE: CIA project targeting Soviet workers in eastern Europe nuclear installations by bouncing microwaves off the ionosphere.

RF-MEDIA: In the event of martial law, RF-MEDIA was developed by the CIA for the possibility of quickly "calming down" the population through electronic, multi-directional subliminal suggestion and programming. Using television and radio communications the signals would be broadcast in the frequency ranges known for their mollifying effect on the human brain. It has been reported the system has now been updated to include the Internet and cellular telephones.

TRIDENT: TRIDENT is believed to have commenced in 1989 as a project by the National Security Agency (NSA). The goal was the electronic directed targeting of individuals or populations, especially assembled groups. Using black helicopters flying in a triad formation, 1000,000 watts of RF in the UHF range was to be used for large group management, behavior and riot control.

SPECIAL REPORT

Mind Control in the 21st Century

New methods of mind control technology were first introduced in the 1950s as an obscure branch of the CIA's MKULTRA project group. Just as organized crime is not stopped by hearings and court cases, neither did this originally obscure branch of MKULTRA activity, when the top secret operations were exposed by the U.S. Senate's Church-Inouye hearings in the late 1970s.

Since government-backed electronic mind control is classified at the highest levels in all technologically capable governments, the description of effects is taken from the personal experiences of over 300 known involuntary experimentees. The experimentees without exception report that once the "testing" begins, the classified experiment specification apparently requires that the "testing" be continued for life. Many test subjects are now in their 70s and 80s. Some have children and the children are often subjected to the same "testing" as their parent(s).

In an amazing article published by Spectra Magazine in 1999, author Rauni-Leena Luukanen-Kilde, MD, Former Chief Medical Officer of Finland, writes that in 1948 Norbert Weiner published a book, Cybernetics, defined as a neurological communication and control theory already in use in small circles at that time. Yoneji Masuda, "Father of the Information Society," stated his concern in 1980 that our liberty is threatened Orwellian-style by cybernetic technology totally unknown to most people. This technology links the brains of people via implanted microchips to satellites controlled by ground-based supercomputers.

The first brain implants were surgically inserted in 1974 in the state of Ohio and also in Stockholm, Sweden. Brain electrodes were inserted into the skulls of babies in 1946 without the knowledge of their parents. In the 1950s and 60s, electrical implants were inserted into the brains of animals and humans, especially in the U.S., during research into behavior modification, and brain and body functioning. Mind control (MC) methods were used in attempts to change human behavior and attitudes. Influencing brain functions became an important goal of military and intelligence services.

Thirty years ago brain implants showed up in X-rays the size of one centimeter. Subsequent implants shrunk to the size of a grain of rice. They were made of silicon, later still of gallium arsenide. Today they are small enough to be inserted into the neck or back, and also intravenously in different parts of the body during surgical operations, with or without the consent of the subject. It is now almost impossible to detect or remove them.

It is technically possible for every newborn to be injected with a microchip, which could then function to identify the person for the rest of his or her life. Such plans are secretly being discussed in the U.S. without any public airing of the privacy issues involved. In Sweden, Prime Minister Olof Palme gave permission in 1973 to implant prisoners, and Data Inspection's ex-Director General Jan Freese revealed that nursing-home patients were implanted in the mid-1980s.

Implanted human beings can be followed anywhere. Their brain functions can be remotely monitored by supercomputers and even altered through the changing of frequencies. Guinea pigs in secret experiments have included prisoners, soldiers, mental patients, handicapped children, deaf and blind people, homosexuals, single women, the elderly, school children, and any group of people considered "marginal" by the elite experimenters. The published experiences of prisoners in Utah State Prison, for example, are shocking to the conscience.

Today's microchips operate by means of low-frequency radio waves that target them. With the help of satellites, the implanted person can be tracked anywhere on the globe. Such a technique was among a number tested in the Iraq war, according to Dr. Carl Sanders, who invented the intelligence-manned interface (IMI) biotic, which is injected into people. (Earlier during the Vietnam War, soldiers were injected with the Rambo chip, designed to increase adrenaline flow into the bloodstream.) The 20-billion-bit/second supercomputers at the U.S. National Security Agency (NSA) could now "see and hear" what soldiers experience in the battlefield with a remote monitoring system (RMS).

When a 5-micromillimeter microchip (the diameter of a strand of hair is 50 micromillimeters) is placed into optical nerve of the eye, it draws neuroimpulses from the brain that embody the experiences, smells, sights, and voice of the implanted person. Once transferred and stored in a computer, these neuroimpulses can be projected back to the person's brain via the microchip to be re-experienced. Using a RMS, a land-based computer operator can send electromagnetic messages (encoded as signals) to the nervous system, affecting the target's performance. With RMS, healthy persons can be induced to see hallucinations and to hear voices in their heads. Every thought, reaction, hearing, and visual observation causes a certain neurological potential, spikes, and patterns in the brain and its electromagnetic fields, which can now be decoded into thoughts, pictures, and voices. Electromagnetic stimulation can therefore change a person's brain-waves and affect muscular activity, causing painful muscular cramps experienced as torture.

The NSA's electronic surveillance system can simultaneously follow and handle millions of people. Each of us has a unique bioelectrical resonance frequency in the brain, just as we have unique fingerprints. With electromagnetic frequency (EMF) brain stimulation fully coded, pulsating electromagnetic signals can be sent to the brain, causing the desired voice and visual effects to be experienced by the target. This is a form of electronic warfare. U.S. astronauts were implanted before they were sent into space so their thoughts could be followed and all their emotions could be registered 24 hours a day.

The Washington Post reported in May 1995 that Prince William of Great Britain was implanted at the age of 12. Thus, if he were ever kidnaped, a radio wave with a specific frequency could be targeted to his microchip. The chip's signal would be routed through a satellite to the computer screen of police headquarters, where the Prince's movements could be followed. He could actually be located anywhere on the globe.

The mass media has not reported that an implanted person's privacy vanishes for the rest of his or her life. S/he can be manipulated in many ways. Using different frequencies, the secret controller of this equipment can even change a person's emotional life. S/he can be made aggressive or lethargic. Sexuality can be artificially influenced. Thought signals and subconscious thinking can be read, dreams affected and even induced, all without the knowledge or consent of the implanted person.

A perfect cyber-soldier can thus be created. This secret technology has been used by military forces in certain NATO countries since the 1980s without civilian and academic populations having heard anything about it. Thus, little information about such invasive mind-control systems is available in professional and academic journals.

The NSA's Signals Intelligence group can remotely monitor information from human brains by decoding the evoked potentials (3.50HZ, 5 milliwatt) emitted by the brain. Prisoner experimentees in both Gothenburg, Sweden and Vienna, Austria have been found to have evident brain lesions. Diminished blood circulation and lack of oxygen in the right temporal frontal lobes result where brain implants are usually operative. A Finnish experimentee experienced brain atrophy and intermittent attacks

MIND STALKERS

of unconsciousness due to lack of oxygen. Mind control techniques can be used for political purposes. The goal of mind controllers today is to induce the targeted persons or groups to act against his or her own convictions and best interests. Zombified individuals can even be programmed to murder and remember nothing of their crime afterward. Alarming examples of this phenomenon can be found in the U.S.

This "silent war" is being conducted against unknowing civilians and soldiers by military and intelligence agencies. Since 1980, electronic stimulation of the brain (ESB) has been secretly used to control people targeted without their knowledge or consent. All international human rights agreements forbid nonconsensual manipulation of human beings — even in prisons, not to speak of civilian populations.

Under an initiative of U.S. Senator John Glenn, discussions commenced in January 1997 about the dangers of radiating civilian populations. Targeting people's brain functions with electromagnetic fields and beams (from helicopters and airplanes, satellites, from parked vans, neighboring houses, telephone poles, electrical appliances, mobile phones, TV, radio, etc.) is part of the radiation problem that should be addressed in democratically elected government bodies.

In addition to electronic MC, chemical methods have also been developed. Mind-altering drugs and different smelling gasses affecting brain function negatively can be injected into air ducts or water pipes. Bacteria and viruses have also been tested this way in several countries.

Today's super-technology, connecting our brain functions via microchips (or even without them, according to the latest technology) to computers via satellites in the U.S. or Israel, poses the gravest threat to humanity. The latest supercomputers are powerful enough to monitor the whole world's population. What will happen when people are tempted by false premises to allow microchips into their bodies? One lure will be a microchip identity card. Compulsory legislation has even been secretly proposed in the U.S. to criminalize removal of an ID implant.

Are we ready for the robotization of mankind and the total elimination of privacy, including freedom of thought? How many of us would want to cede our entire life, including our most secret thoughts, to Big Brother? Yet the technology exists to create a totalitarian New World Order. Covert neurological communication systems are in place to counteract independent thinking and to control social and political activity on behalf of self-serving private and military interests.

137

MIND STALKERS

When our brain functions are already connected to supercomputers by means of radio implants and microchips, it will be too late for protest. This threat can be defeated only by educating the public, using available literature on biotelemetry and information exchanged at international congresses.

One reason this technology has remained a state secret is the widespread prestige of the Psychiatric Diagnostic Statistical Manual IV produced by the U.S. American Psychiatric Association (APA) and printed in 18 languages. Psychiatrists working for U.S. intelligence agencies no doubt participated in writing and revising this manual. This psychiatric "bible" covers up the secret development of MC technologies by labeling some of their effects as symptoms of paranoid schizophrenia.

Victims of mind control experimentation are thus routinely diagnosed, knee-jerk fashion, as mentally ill by doctors who learned the DSM "symptom" list in medical school. Physicians have not been schooled that patients may be telling the truth when they report being targeted against their will or being used as guinea pigs for electronic, chemical and bacteriological forms of psychological warfare.

POWER OF THE MILITARY-INDUSTRIAL COMPLEX

Jan Wiesemann has written an apt description of the situation which now exists in the United States, about the 'forces that be' and how the situation came about:

"During the Cold War the United States not only engaged in a relatively open nuclear arms race with the Soviet Union, but also engaged in a secret race developing unconventional mind control weapons. As the intelligence agencies (which prior to the Second World War had merely played a supporting role within the government) continued to increase their power, so did the funds spent on developing techniques designed to outsmart each other.

"And as the U.S. intelligence community began to grow, a secret culture sprang about which enabled the intelligence players to implement the various developed techniques to cleverly circumvent the democratic processes and institutions...

"Like many other democracies, the U.S. Government is made up of two basic parts the elected constituency, i.e., the various governors, judges, congressmen and the President; and the unelected bureaucracies, as represented by the numerous federal agencies.

MIND STALKERS

"In a well-balanced and correctly functioning democracy, the elected part of the government is in charge of its unelected bureaucratic part, giving the people a real voice in the agenda set by their government.

"While a significant part of the U.S. Government no doubt follows this democratic principle, a considerable portion of the U.S. Government operates in complete secrecy and follows its own unaccountable agenda which, unacknowledged, very often is quite different from the public agenda."

The secrecy involved in the development of the electromagnetic mind control technology reflects the tremendous power that is inherent in it. To put it bluntly, whoever controls this technology can control the minds of everyone.

There is evidence that the U.S. Government has plans to extend the range of this technology to envelop all peoples, all countries. This can be accomplished, is being accomplished, by using the HAARP Project for overseas areas and the GWEN network now in place in the U.S.

Dr Michael Persinger, Professor of Psychology and Neuroscience at Laurentian University, Ontario, Canada, has discovered through intensive research that strong electromagnetic fields can affect a person's brain.

"Temporal lobe stimulation," he says, "can evoke the feeling of a presence, disorientation, and perceptual irregularities. It can activate images stored in the subject's memory, including nightmares and monsters that are normally suppressed."

Dr Persinger wrote an article a few years ago, titled : *On the Possibility of Directly Accessing Every Human Brain by Electromagnetic Induction of Fundamental Algorithms*. The abstract reads:

"Contemporary neuroscience suggests the existence of fundamental algorithms by which all sensory transduction is translated into an intrinsic, brain-specific code. Direct stimulation of these codes within the human temporal or limbic cortices by applied electromagnetic patterns may require energy levels which are within the range of both geomagnetic activity and contemporary communication networks. A process which is coupled to the narrow band of brain temperature could allow all normal human brains to be. affected by a subharmonic whose frequency range at about 10 Hz would only vary by 0. 1 Hz."

"Within the last two decades a potential has emerged which was improbable, but which is now marginally feasible. This potential is the technical capability to influence directly the major portion of the approximately six billion brains of the human species, without mediation through classical sensory modalities, by generating neural information within a physical medium within which all members of the species are immersed.

"The historical emergence of such possibilities, which have ranged from gunpowder to atomic fission, have resulted in major changes in the social evolution that occurred inordinately quickly after the implementation. Reduction of the risk of the inappropriate application of these technologies requires the continued and open discussion of their realistic feasibility and implications within the scientific and public domain."

INFLUENCE FROM ABOVE: MIND CONTROL SATELLITES

Unknown to most of the world, satellites can perform astonishing and often menacing feats. This should come as no surprise when one reflects on the massive effort poured into satellite technology since the Soviet satellite Sputnik, launched in 1957, caused panic in the U.S. A spy satellite can monitor a person's every movement, even when the "target" is indoors or deep in the interior of a building or traveling rapidly down the highway in a car, in any kind of weather (cloudy, rainy, stormy). There is no place to hide on the face of the earth.

It takes just three satellites to blanket the world with detection capacity. Besides tracking a person's every action and relaying the data to a computer screen on earth, amazing powers of satellites include reading a person's mind, monitoring conversations, manipulating electronic instruments and physically assaulting someone with a laser beam. Remote reading of someone's mind through satellite technology is quite bizarre, yet it is being done; it is a reality

It is difficult to estimate just how many people world wide are being watched by satellites, but if there are 200 working surveillance satellites (a common number in the literature), and if each satellite can monitor 20 human targets, then as many as 4000 people may be under satellite surveillance. However, the capability of a satellite for multiple-target monitoring is even harder to estimate than the number of satellites; it may be connected to the number of transponders on each satellite, the transponder being a key device for both receiving and transmitting information.

A society in the grips of the National Security State is necessarily kept in the dark about such things. Obviously, though, if one satellite can monitor simultaneously 40 or 80 human targets, then the number of possible victims of satellite surveillance would be doubled or quadrupled. As early as 1981, G. Harry Stine (in his book

MIND STALKERS

Confrontation in Space), could write that Computers have read human minds by means of deciphering the outputs of electroencephalographs (EEGs). Early work in this area was reported by the Defense Advanced Research Projects Agency (DARPA) in 1978. EEG's are now known to be crude sensors of neural activity in the human brain, depending as they do upon induced electrical currents in the skin.

In 1992, *Newsweek* reported that "with powerful new devices that peer through the skull and see the brain at work, neuroscientists seek the wellsprings of thoughts and emotions, the genesis of intelligence and language. They hope, in short, to read your mind." In 1994, a scientist noted that "current imaging techniques can depict physiological events in the brain which accompany sensory perception and motor activity, as well as cognition and speech."

In order to give a satellite mind-reading capability, it only remains to put some type of EEG-like-device on a satellite and link it with a computer that has a data bank of brain-mapping research. I believe that surveillance satellites began reading minds--or rather, began allowing the minds of targets to be read--sometime in the early 1990s. Some satellites in fact can read a person's mind from space.

A surveillance satellite, in addition, can detect human speech. Burrows observed that satellites can "even eavesdrop on conversations taking place deep within the walls of the Kremlin." Walls, ceilings, and floors are no barrier to the monitoring of conversation from space. Even if you were in a high rise building with ten stories above you and ten stories below, a satellite's audio surveillance of your speech would still be unhampered. Inside or outside, in any weather, anyplace on earth, at any time of day, a satellite in a geosynchronous orbit can detect the speech of a human target. Apparently, as with reconnaissance in general, only by taking cover deep within the bowels of a lead-shielding fortified building could you escape audio monitoring by a satellite.

There are various other satellite powers, such as manipulating electronic instruments and appliances like alarms, electronic watches and clocks, a television, radio, smoke detector and the electrical system of an automobile. For example, the digital alarm on a watch, tiny though it is, can be set off by a satellite from hundreds of miles up in space. And the light bulb of a lamp can be burned out with the burst of a laser from a satellite. In addition, street lights and porch lights can be turned on and off at will by someone at the controls of a satellite, the means being an electromagnetic beam which reverses the light's polarity. Or a lamp can be made to burn out in a burst of blue light when the switch is flicked.   As with other satellite powers, it makes no difference if the light is under a roof or a ton of concrete – it can still be manipulated by a satellite laser. Types of satellite lasers include the free-electron laser, the x-ray laser, the neutral-particle-beam laser, the chemical-oxygen-iodine laser and the mid-infra-red advanced chemical laser.

Along with mind-reading, one of the most bizarre uses of a satellite is to physically assault someone. An electronic satellite beam--using far less energy than needed to blast nuclear missiles in flight – can "slap" or bludgeon someone on earth. A satellite beam can also be locked onto a human target, with the victim being unable to evade the menace by running around or driving around, and can cause harm through application of pressure on, for example, one's head. How severe a beating can be administered from space is a matter of conjecture, but if the ability to actually murder someone this way has not yet been worked out, there can be no doubt that it will soon become a reality. There is no mention in satellite literature of a murder having been committed through the agency of a satellite, but the very possibility should make the world take note.

There is yet another macabre power possessed by some satellites: manipulating a person's mind with an audio subliminal "message" (a sound too low for the ear to consciously detect but which affects the unconscious). In trying thereby to get a person to do what you want him to do, it does not matter if the target is asleep or awake. A message could be used to compel a person to say something you would like him to say, in a manner so spontaneous that no one would be able to realize the words were contrived by someone else; there is no limit to the range of ideas an unsuspecting person can be made to voice.

The human target might be compelled to use an obscenity, or persons around the target might be compelled to say things that insult the target. A sleeping person, on the other hand, is more vulnerable and can be made to do something, rather than merely say something. An action compelled by an audio subliminal message could be to roll off the bed and fall onto the floor, or to get up and walk around in a trance. However, the sleeping person can only be made to engage in such an action for only a minute or so, it seems, since he usually wakes up by then and the spell wears.

It should be noted here that although the hypnotism of a psychoanalyst is bogus, unconscious or subconscious manipulation of behavior is genuine. But the brevity of a subliminal spell effected by a satellite might be overcome by more research. "The psychiatric community," reported *Newsweek* in 1994, "generally agrees that subliminal perception exists; a smaller fringe group believes it can be used to change the psyche."

SCIENTIST CONFIRMS REALITY OF ELECTRONIC MIND CONTROL

A Russian doctor, Igor Smirnov, whom the magazine labeled a "subliminal Dr. Strangelove," is one scientist studying the possibilities: "Using electroencephalographs, he measures brain waves, then uses computers to create a map of the subconscious and various human impulses, such as anger or the sex drive. Then, through taped subliminal messages, he claims to physically alter that landscape with the power of suggestion."

In the August 22, 1994 issue of *Newsweek*, Dr. Smirnov revealed that the FBI asked advice from Smirnov during the siege at Waco. Smirnov said that: "The FBI wanted to 'pipe subliminal messages from sect member's families through the telephone lines into the compound."

For David Koresh the group's leader... the FBI had in mind a special voice: "God as played by the famous actor Charlton Heston."

In this case the sect members would be influenced by electromagnetic high frequency voices of their relatives, and David Koresh would hear in his head the voice of God played by Charlton Heston. Smirnov told the FBI that they would have to find the individual frequencies of the sect members if the idea was to work correctly.

Combining this research with satellite technology – which has already been done in part – could give its masters the possibility for the perfect crime, since satellites operate with perfect discretion, perfect concealment. In many countries the military operates tracking stations; assisting the giant American National Security Agency. The NSA covertly monitors every call, fax, e-mail, telex and computer data message. The relevant computers search for key words/phrases. Anything/anyone of interest is drawn to the attention of agency operatives. This can lead to a large scale personal surveillance operation by the NSA or other agencies; like the CIA and their criminal connections. The current system is called ECHELON.

The magnetic field around the head is scanned as you are satellite tracked. The results are then fed back to the relevant computers. Monitors then use the information to conduct a conversation where audible neurophone input is applied to the victim. The neurophone was developed by Dr Patrick Flanagan in 1958. It's a device that converts sound to electrical impulses. In its original form electrodes were placed on the skin but with defense department developments, the signals can be delivered via satellite. They then travel the nervous system directly to the brain (bypassing normal hearing mechanisms). Dr. Flanagan's 3D holographic sound system can place sounds in any location as perceived by the targeted / tortured listener. This allows for a variety of deceptions for gullible victims.

Today, various top secret groups use satellites and ground based equipment to deliver verbal threats, deafening noise and propaganda; using neurophone technology. Anything from TV's/radio's appearing to operate when switched off through to "Voices from God" and encounters with aliens are all cons using neurophone technologies to torment, deceive and (most importantly) discredit agency/criminal targets. Naturally, the system can mimic anyone's voice and automatic computer translations (into any language) are incorporated.

Human thought operates at 5,000 bits/sec but satellites and various forms of biotelemetry can deliver those thoughts to supercomputers located worldwide that have a speed of 20 BILLION bits/sec. These, even today, monitor thousands of people simultaneously. Eventually they will monitor almost everyone.

Usually the targets are aware their brain waves are being monitored because of the accompanying neurophone feedback. In other words, the computer repeats (echoes) your own thoughts and then the human monitors comment or respond verbally. Both are facilitated by the neurophone.

There is little time left to make the rest of the world aware of the nefarious operations now in effect. Our rights and freedoms as human beings are in jeopardy if these warnings continue to go unheeded.

Mind Stalkers

MILABS - The Mind Control UFO Connection

Since the 1960's (and possibly even earlier), some witnesses to UFO events have reported that they were abducted by the alleged alien pilots. In the 1970's these other-worldly kidnappings entered the once-supposed sanctity of the home as people reported being taken from their beds against their will in the middle of the night.

These abduction reports followed a very predictable pattern: a person, or even several people, is taken from their car or home by small, humanoid creatures that are gray in color, have large jet-black eyes and almost no nose, mouth or ears. The abductees are usually given physical exams that are often painful and humiliating. Sometimes there is some form of communication where the abductee is shown images, often apocalyptic in nature. But just as often there is no communication, giving the abductee the impression of being experimented on like a lab animal by unfeeling technicians.

Even more disturbing is the fact that most abductees say that these abductions are not a one-time-only occurrence, as they are taken for experiments numerous times throughout their lives. Frighteningly, children of abductees are also more prone to report abduction experiences of their own more often than children whose parents have not had abductions.

Some researchers have uncovered evidence that some abductees are also being targeted by a group, or groups, that are not from outer space, but from planet Earth. Investigator Helmut Lammer has noted that UFO abductions are generally a very strange and complex phenomenon, and that it has gotten even stranger as some UFO abductees have reported that they have also been kidnapped by human military intelligence personnel (MILAB) and taken to hospitals and/or military facilities, some of which are described as being underground.

Very few of the popular books on the subject of UFO abductions have mentioned these experiences. Especially odd is the fact that abductees recall seeing military intelligence personnel together with alien beings, working side by side in these secret facilities. The presence of human military and civilian personnel occupying the same physical reality as alien beings exceeds the mind-sets of the skeptics and the open-minded researchers by several orders of magnitude. The skeptics would rather believe that stories of aliens and military personnel in governmental underground facilities are fabrications designed to elicit attention from conspiracy believers or hallucinations in general.

Researchers in the field of mind control suggest that these cases are evidence that the whole UFO abduction phenomenon is staged by the intelligence community as a cover for their illegal experiments. The open-minded researchers who are trying to gain respect for abduction research ignore these stories, since they represent only a minor fraction of the cases in their files. Abduction cases involving reports of being taken by the military as well as alien beings are very important for two reasons:

1. If the UFO community has evidence that a covert military intelligence task force is involved in the abduction phenomenon, we would know that this phenomenon represents a matter of national security.

2. The alleged military involvement in the abduction phenomenon could be evidence that the military uses abductees for mind control experiments as test-targets for microwave

weapons. Moreover, the military could be monitoring and even kidnapping abductees for information gathering purposes during, before and after a UFO abduction.

Even though the CIA claims that they stopped all mind control research in the 1970s, it is foolish to think that decades of successful research would be thrown away so cavalierly. What is more likely is that the research and implementation of human mind control has been covered up and compartmentalized to such an extent that only those who are "in the loop" have any knowledge of what is really going on. There are, however, some tantalizing clues on the frightening direction that these underground groups have taken in their quest for the ultimate control of the human mind.

The largest newspaper in Scandinavia, **Helsingin Sanomat**, wrote in the September 9, 1999 issue that **Scientific American** magazine estimates that in the 21st century, perhaps all people will be implanted with a "DNA microchip." How many people realize what it actually means? Total loss of privacy and total outside control of the person's physical body functions, mental, emotional and thought processes, including the implanted person's subconscious and dreams, for the rest of his life.

It sounds like science fiction, but it is secret military and intelligence agencies' mind control technology, which has been experimented with for almost half a century, totally without the knowledge of the general public and even the general academic population.

Supercomputers in Maryland, Israel and elsewhere with a speed of over 20 billion bits/sec can monitor millions of people simultaneously. In fact, the whole world population can be totally controlled by these secret brain-computer interactions, however unbelievable it sounds for the uninformed.

Human thought has a speed of 5,000 bits/sec and everyone understands that our brain cannot compete with supercomputers acting via satellites, implants, local facilities, scalar or other forms of biotelemetry.

Each brain has a unique set of bioelectric resonance/entrainment characteristics. Remote neural monitoring systems with supercomputers can send messages through an implanted person's nervous system and affect their performance in any way desired. They can of course be tracked and identified anywhere.

Neuro-electromagnetic involuntary human experimentation has been going on with the so-called "vulnerable population" for about 50 years, in the name of "science" or "national security" in the worst Nazi-type testing, contrary to all human rights. Physical and psychological torture of mind control victims today is like the worst horror movies. Only, unlike the horror movies, it is true.

It happens today in the United States, Russia, China, Japan, and Europe. With few exceptions, the mass media suppresses all information about the entire topic. Mind control technology in the U.S. is classified under "non-lethal" weaponry. The name is totally misleading because the technology used is lethal, but death comes slowly in the form of "normal" illnesses, like cancer, leukemia, heart attacks, Alzheimer's disease with loss of short term memory first. No wonder these illnesses have increased all over the world. When the use of electromagnetic fields, extra-low (ELF) and ultra-low (ULF) frequencies and microwaves aimed deliberately at certain individuals, groups, and even the general population to cause diseases, disorientation, chaos and physical and emotional pain breaks into the awareness of the general population, a public outcry is inevitable.

Mind Stalkers

Reports from persons targeted by neuroelectromagnetic experimentation show that not everyone is implanted. The fact that those few victims who have had implants removed cannot get custody of the implants means someone has a keen interest in controlling the use of covert implants and preventing the publication of this practice.

Who is behind a sinister plan to microchip and control and torture the general population? The Patent Office of the U.S has granted patents for purposes of mental monitoring and mind alteration.

Apparatus and method for remotely monitoring and altering brainwaves, methods for inducing mental, emotional and physical states of consciousness, in human beings. Method of and apparatus for desired states of consciousness are among some of them.

People who have been implanted, involuntarily or through deception voluntarily have become biological robots and guinea pigs for this activity under the guise of national security. The real consequences of microchip implantation (or with today's advanced hidden technology, using only microwave radiation for mind control,) are totally hidden from the public. How many know the real dangers of microwaves through mobile phones?

How many believe the disinformation that microwave radiation is not causing health problems? The economic issues in the mobile phone industry are enormous. Therefore health issues are deliberately brushed aside.

However, the same thing is inevitable in the future as with the tobacco industry. When economic compensation for health damages becomes big enough, as in the tobacco industry, health hazards will be admitted and users are then responsible for their tobacco-related illnesses.

Cell phones used in mind control was a brilliant idea. Military and police agencies can follow every user, influence their thoughts through microwaves, cause healthy people to hear voices in their heads and if needed burn their brains in a second by increasing the current 20,000 times.

That probably happened to Chechnyan leader General Dudayev who died talking on a cell phone. Heating effect of tissues with the speed of light is a known effect of high power microwave and electromagnetic pulse weapons.

According to Navy studies they also cause fatigue states, depression, insomnia, aggressiveness, long and especially short term memory loss, short catatonic states, cataracts, leukemia, cancer, heart attacks, brain tumors and so forth. Alteration of behavior and attitudes has been demonstrated as well.

Dr. Ross Adey has found out that by using 0.75 milliwatts per square centimeter intensity of pulse modulated microwave at a frequency of 450 MHz it is possible to control ALL aspects of human behavior.

Microwave radiation excites the hydrogen bond in the cells and can interfere with meiosis, which leads to tumors. All our emotions, moods, and thoughts have a specific brain frequency which has been catalogued. If these records fall into the wrong hands, our behavior and attitudes can be manipulated by persons whose ethics and morals are not in our best interest.

Both military and intelligence agencies have been infiltrated with such persons. The Director of the Swiss Secret Service had to resign in September 1999 because of his agency's involvement in illegal arms deals and a plan to create an organization within the

Mind Stalkers

legal Secret Service. This globally infiltrated organization has "octopus type" activities in all major intelligence services in the world, working together with the Mafia and terrorists. It has recruited people from all important government institutions, state and local administrations.

It owns Star Wars technology which is used against military and civilian populations, claiming it is "non-lethal" weaponry. "Down and out" people, jobless, freed prisoners, mental outpatients, students and orphans are trained by this organization to harass, follow, and torture innocent people, who for whatever reason have been put on the organization's hit list. They are already in every neighborhood.

Deception is the name of the game, so recruits are told untrue sinister stories of their victims to keep them motivated. The media, large corporations, religious and political leaders are also infiltrated.

Who are the targets? Experimentation with soldiers and prisoners may continue, as well as handicapped children, UFO witnesses, mental patients, homosexuals and single women. However, anyone can become a target, even those who invented the system.

Researchers who find out about this secret radiation of the population become targets themselves. The U.S. Senate discussed the issue on January 22, 1997. The U.S. Air Force's "Commando Solo" aircraft have been used to send subliminal radio frequency messages to manipulate even the minds of foreign nations in their elections. Haiti, Bosnia and Iraq are a couple of recent examples.

In July 1994 the U.S. Department of Defense proposed the use of "non-lethal" weapons against anyone engaged in activities the DoD opposes. Thus opposing political views, economic competitors, counterculture individuals and so forth can be beamed to sickness or death.

The Psychiatric Diagnostic Statistical Manual (DSM) for mental disorders has been a brilliant cover up operation in 18 languages to hide the atrocities of military and intelligence agencies' actions towards their targets. The manual lists all mind control actions as signs of paranoid schizophrenia.

If a target is under surveillance with modern technology via TV, radio, telephone, loudspeakers, lasers, microwaves, poisoned with mind altering drugs via airducts, giving familiar smells which cause headache, nausea and so forth, if he claims his clothes are poisoned, his food or tap water as well – all medical schools teach their students that the person is paranoid, especially if he believes the government, intelligence agencies, or UFOs are behind it all.

Never is the medical profession told that these are routine actions all over the world by intelligence agencies against their targets. Thus, victims of mind control are falsely considered mentally ill and get no help since they are not believed and their suffering is doubled by ignorant health professionals.

The unethical abuses of power by individuals in charge of biomedical telemetry are incomprehensible to normal people. The goal of mind control is to program an individual to carry out any mission of espionage or assassination even against their will and self-preservation instinct and to control the absolute behavior and thought patterns of the individual. The purpose of mind control is to disrupt memory, discredit people through aberrant behavior, to make them insane or to commit suicide or murder. How is it possible that this technology is not stopped by political top authorities? They themselves will also be targets someday, a fact they have not always realized. How much are they involved?

After the 9/11 terrorist attacks, the U.S. congress gave carte blanche approval to President Bush's notorious Patriot Act, this despite the fact that few lawmakers were even allowed to read the act and the attack on civil liberties its approval would allow. Many congressmen stated after the fact that they could not explain why they voted for the Patriot Acts approval.

In fact, in 2006, congress once again voted to extend the Patriot Act, even though most of the countries voters were dead-set against the draconian measures allowed within it. It was as is the countries lawmakers had no will of their own.

In recent years, various information on remote mind control technology has filtered into the conspiracy research community through such publications such as Conspiracy Journal, as well as a Finnish gentleman by the name of Martti Koski and his booklet *My Life Depends On You*. Over the last decade, Koski has been sharing his horrifying tale, documenting the discovery of rampant brain tampering committed upon himself and countless others.

The perpetrators of these evil doings allegedly include the Royal Canadian Mounted Police (RCMP), The CIA and Finnish Intelligence, among various other intelligence agencies. At one point during a mind control programming episode, the "doctors" operating on Koski identified themselves as "aliens from Sirius." Apparently, these "doctors" were attempting to plant a screen memory to conceal their true intentions.

What this suggests is a theory that alien abductions were a cover for MK-ULTRA mind control experiments perpetrated by secret intelligence agencies.

According to author Walter Bowart in the revised edition of *Operation Mind Control*, one alleged mind control victim said that in the late 70's the victim had been the recipient of a mock alien abduction, the intention of which was to create a screen memory that would conceal the actual mind control programs enacted on the victim. The subject in this instance claimed to have seen a young child dressed in a small alien costume, similar in appearance to the aliens in Steven Spielberg's movie *ET*.

None of this, of course, dismisses outright the theory that UFOs are alien spacecraft. Nevertheless, its implications are staggering when one considers the impact and subsequent commercialization of the alien abduction phenomenon, and how it has reshaped the belief systems and psyches of millions upon millions of the planet's inhabitants, in essence creating a new paradigm on the reality of visitors from other planets that prior to thirty years ago was virtually non-existent.

As chronicled in Walter Bowart's *Operation Mind Control*, in the late 70's Congressman Charlie Rose (D-N.C) met with a Canadian inventor who had developed a helmet that simulated alternate states of consciousness and realities. One such virtual reality scenario played out by those who tried on this helmet was a mock alien abduction.

Congressman Rose took part in these experiments, which consisted of the alien abduction program. Much to Rose's amazement, the simulated scenario seemed incredibly realistic. This device sounds quite similar to Dr. Michael Persinger's much-touted "Magic Helmet," which has been receiving a fair amount of press in recent years. Equipped with magnets that beam a low-level magnetic field at the temporal lobe, the "Helmet" effects areas of brain associated with time distortions and other altered states of consciousness. Although Bowart did not specifically name the inventor of the helmet in *Operation Mind Control*, chances are it was Persinger to whom he was referring. Persinger's name has also been bandied about by mind control researcher, Martin Cannon – in his treatise *The Controllers* – as a behind the scenes player in intelligence operations related to MK-ULTRA.

This takes us back to Helmut Lammer and his Project MILAB. His studies indicate that MILAB abductees are harassed by dark, unmarked helicopters that fly around their houses. Lammer has discovered that the helicopter activity associated with UFO abductions has increased from the eighties to the present day. Dan Wright has ten cases in the MUFON Transcription Project files where helicopters were seen flying in the area of the abductee's home within hours of an alleged UFO abduction. Lammer has also found that many abduction researchers in North America have, on average, about three helicopter cases connected with UFO abductions in their files.

Most abductees report interaction with military intelligence personnel after the helicopters begin to appear. Debbie Jordan reports, for instance, in a side note of her book *Abducted!* that she was stunned by an alleged friend and taken to a kind of hospital where she was examined by a medical doctor. This doctor removed an implant from her ear.

The abduction experiences of Leah Haley and Ms. K. Wilson are full of MILAB encounters. Some of Ms. Wilson's experiences are comparable with mind control experiments. For example, she writes of a flashback from her childhood where she remembers being forced into what appears to be a Skinner Box-like container which may have been used for behavior modification purposes.

Because of these types of experiences, Ms. Wilson published an article on her web site titled *Project Open Mind: Are Some Alien Abductions Government Mind Control Experiments?* Beth Collins and Anna Jamerson included hypnosis transcripts of an abduction by human military personnel in their book *Connections*, and the late Dr. Karla Turner investigated MILABs in her books: *Into the Fringe* and *Taken: Inside the Alien-Human Abduction Agenda*.

Lammer reports that MILABs involve the following elements: Dark, unmarked helicopter activity, the appearance of strange vans or buses outside the houses of abductees, exposure to disorienting electromagnetic fields, drugging, and transport by a helicopter, bus or truck to an unknown building or an underground military facility. Usually after the military kidnappings, there are physical after effects such as grogginess and sometimes nausea.

There is also a difference when the abductors appear. In most UFO abduction cases, the beings appear through a closed window, wall, or the abductee feels a strange presence in the room. Most abductees report that they are paralyzed from the mental power of the alien beings.

During MILABs the abductee reports that the kidnappers give him or her a shot with a syringe. It is also interesting that MILAB abductees report that they are examined by human doctor's in rectangular rooms and not in round sterile rooms, as they are described during most UFO abductions. The described rooms, halls and furniture are similar to terrestrial hospital rooms, laboratories or research facilities and have nothing to do with "UFO" furniture.

Mind Stalkers

During a MILAB, the examination is similar as during UFO abductions. However, the MILAB victim is not paralyzed, but rather, tied to an examination table or a gynecological chair. Sometimes, the abductee gets a strong drink before the examination. This is perhaps a contrast-enhancing fluid.

MILAB doctors are usually dressed in white lab coats and show an interest in implants as well as gynecological examinations. In some MILAB cases military doctors searched for implants and sometimes even implanted the abductee with a military device. Therefore, surgeons extracting alleged alien implants should be prepared in the event they find military devices since human implant technology is very advanced.

It should be considered that some of the information received from MILAB abductees may be cover stories, induced by the hypno-programming processes of military psychiatrists. There is also the possibility that the military uses rubber alien masks and special effects during a MILAB.

Facts such as these lead some mind control researchers to believe that all alien abductees are used in secret mind control and/or genetic experiments staged by a powerful black arm of the United States government. However, investigators should not jump to any conclusions until all of the facts are in. Serious researchers should investigate all possibilities. Some UFO abductees may indeed be mind control victims or they may have been used in black-ops genetic experiments from the eighties or earlier.

Lammer speculates that the alien/human abduction scenario is more complex than previously thought. It seems that there is evidence that more than one human agenda may be involved in the unexplained alien abduction phenomenon. Each of these agendas probably has their own interest in alleged alien abductees.

It also seems that the first group is interested in mind and behavior control experiments. There is evidence of sensory deprivation experiments, liquid breathing experiments, experiments on electromagnetic stimulation of the temporal lobes, brain research and implant research.

The second group seems to be interested in biological and/or genetic research. Some MILAB victims recall that they saw humans in tubes filled with liquid and genetically altered animals in cages during their kidnappings inside military underground facilities. It should be noted that alien abductees "without" military contacts remember similar scenarios inside UFOs.

The third group seems to be a military task force, which operates since the eighties and is interested in the UFO/alien abduction phenomenon for information gathering purposes. This would be a logical consequence if one with the right "Need to Know" considers that some alien abductions may be real.

It could be that the leaders of this military task force think that some alien abductions are real and that they have national security implications. It could be that the second and third group works together, since they could share their interest in genetic studies and findings from alleged alien abductees.

In a recent paper published for the Air Force 2025 study with the title *Information Operations: A new War-Fighting Capability*, the authors write about a brain implanted cyber situation. In this paper the authors propagate implanted microscopic brain chips which perform two functions: The bio-chip connects the implanted individual to a constellation of integrated or smart satellites (IIC) in low earth orbit, creating an interface between the implanted person and the information resources. The implant relays the processed information from the IIC to the user.

Second, the bio-chip creates a computer generated mental visualization based upon the user's request. The visualization encompasses the individual and allows the user to place him into a selected "battle space." Further a wide range of lethal or non-lethal weapons will be linked to the IIC, allowing special authorized implanted users (super-cyber-soldiers) to directly employ these weapons. This means, a soldier sees the normal world plus an overlay of information identifying and describing specific objects in his field of view. He can now evaluate the threat these targets represent and order a variety of weapon systems to engage and destroy these targets from the distant.

One can see from such military studies that secret research in human-brain-machine and virtual reality implant research is going on. Most of the references in this paper refer to military research institutes and are classified for the public. Since the authors write that implanting things in peoples raises ethical and public relation issues today, one should ask where the guinea pigs of these futuristic research projects are.

MILABs could be evidence that a secret military intelligence task force has been operating in North America since the early eighties, and is involved in the monitoring and kidnapping of alleged UFO abductees. They monitor the houses of their victims, kidnap and possibly implant them with military devices shortly after a UFO abduction experience. It appears that they are searching for possible alien implants as well. Their gynecological interest in female abductees could be explained if they are searching for alleged alien-hybrid embryos. One thing is certain, this task force and the people who are behind these kidnappings are using advanced mind control technology which is currently being tested illegally on individuals who have nothing to do with UFO abductions.

The Voice of God

Through most of human history there has been a series of efforts by some people to control what other people think. The notion that the human mind could be influenced by an outside source was popularized by Edward Hunter in his 1951 book: ***Brainwashing in Red China***. During the Korean War, American prisoners renounced their citizenship in radio broadcasts and many signed confessions against American interests, including charges, still debated today, that the United States was engaged in germ warfare with anthrax.

Careful investigation has uncovered evidence that modern research and experiments in the field of mind control go as far back (and probably farther) as World War II. It was revealed in 1977 through a Senate subcommittee on Health and Scientific Research, chaired by Senator Ted Kennedy, that in 1953, CIA director Allen Dulles distinguished two fronts in the then-current "battle for men's minds;" a "first front" of mass indoctrination through censorship and propaganda, and a "second front" of individual "brainwashing" and "brain changing."

From this came the secret mind control research and development program MK-ULTRA, which had grown out of an earlier program known as Bluebird, created to counter Soviet advances in brainwashing. In reality the CIA had other objectives. An earlier aim was to study methods in which control of an individual could be attained. As well, the CIA was also interested in being able to manipulate foreign leaders through mind control.

The early MK-ULTRA experiments focused on drugs such as LSD and other narcotics. However, it soon became clear to CIA scientists that drugs had their limitations. Because of this, attention was shifted to other methods of mind control, especially electronics.

Doctors have long recognized that the human brain can be influenced by a myriad of outside influences. Yet few people realize that the brain can be manipulated by such things as bright, flashing lights, to implants, microwaves and other "beamed" electronic sources. Because of this evidence, the stereotypical image of the mentally ill person who complains that the government is beaming messages into their brain, might not be so far-fetched after all.

VOICES IN YOUR HEAD

In late 2007 People walking down Prince Street in Soho was shocked to hear a woman's voice whisper right in their ear asking, "Who's there? Who's there?" only to find no one close by. Then the voice said, "It's not your imagination."

Some may think that they have suffered a mental collapse, while others may attribute the strange voice to the supernatural. However, before anyone calls a doctor or a priest they should know that they have just experienced an amazing form of advertising for the A&E series *Paranormal State*.

Overlooking the street is a billboard that uses technology manufactured by the company Holosonics Research Labs, Inc. The ad transmits an "audio spotlight" from a rooftop speaker so that the sound is contained within your cranium. The technology, ideal for situations that require a quiet setting, has rarely been used on such a scale before.

For those who unwittingly walk within the narrow beam, the advertisement can be an unsettling experience, especially if they do not make the connection between the voice and the billboard.

Joe Pompei, president and founder of Holosonics, said the creepy approach is key to drawing attention to A&E's show. But, he noted, the technology was designed to avoid adding to noise pollution. Holosonics AudioSpotlight controls sound like a laser controls a beam of light, sound only goes where it is aimed. Using ultrasound, whose wavelengths are only a few millimeters long, the technology projects a narrow beam of sound that can shine, scatter and reflect similar to light. The beam of sound is so precise that someone standing just inches outside of it would hear nothing.

As the ultrasonic beam travels through the air, the inherent properties of the air cause the ultrasound to change shape in a predictable way. This distortion gives rise to frequency components in the audible bandwidth, which can be accurately predicted, and precisely controlled. By generating the correct ultrasonic signal, any sound desired can be created within the air itself.

The technique of using a nonlinear interaction of high-frequency waves to generate low-frequency waves was originally pioneered by researchers developing underwater sonar techniques dating back to the 1960s. There is evidence taken from the CIA's mind control project MK-ULTRA that ultrasound was researched and developed as far back as the late 1950s. The few remaining papers referring to ultrasound research suggest that the technology was possibly developed to project voices to make someone think they were going insane. As well, it was considered as a method to deliver messages directly to an agent in the field without being noticed by an enemy.

It is probably no coincidence that many people who claim to be unwitting guinea pigs for mind control research have reported hearing voices similar to the voices projected by the AudioSpotlight.

GOD TOLD ME TO DO IT

The technique of using ultrasonics to influence the human mind is also being used by the U.S. military in Iraq. Categorized as a non-lethal system, LRAD (Long Range Acoustic Device), originally had been designed to emit a very loud sound. Anyone whose head was touched by this beam, heard a painful noise. Anyone standing next to them heard nothing. But those hit by the beam promptly fled, or fell to the ground in pain.

LRAD was recently used off Somalia, by a cruise ship, to repel pirates. Some U.S. Navy ships also carry the device, but not just to repel attacking suicide bombers. LRAD can also broadcast speech for up to half a mile.

The navy planned to use LRAD to warn ships to get out of the way. This was needed in places like the crowded coastal waters of the northern Persian Gulf, where the navy patrols. With LRAD, you just aim it at a member of the crew, and have an interpreter "speak" to the sailor.

It was noted that the guy on the receiving end was sometimes terrified, even after he realized it was that large American destroyer that was talking to him. This apparently gave the military some ideas, for there are now rumors in Iraq of an American weapon that makes' people believe they are hearing voices in their heads.

It appears that some of the troops in Iraq are using LRAD to terrify enemy fighters. Using the Islamic terrorist's religious beliefs against them, American troops use the LRAD to put the "word of God" into the heads of insurgents. If God, in the form of a voice that only you can hear, tells you to surrender, or run away, the outcome is quite predictable.

The ability to remotely transmit voices into a target's head is known inside the Pentagon as "Synthetic Telepathy." According to Dr. Robert Becker in his 1998 book **The Body Electric**, "Synthetic Telepathy has applications in covert operations designed to drive a target crazy with voices or deliver undetected instructions to a programmed assassin."

What is especially frightening about the use of such technology is that it does not take a large leap of faith to consider that synthetic telepathy is already being used in the United States, and more than likely, other countries, to control and influence the population. As well, considering that certain political leaders say that they often hear to voice of God directing them to do things such as attack other countries, it is clear that no one is safe from the ravages of mind control.

So the next time you read a rambling letter from someone claiming that the government is beaming "mind control" rays into their brains - you may want to reconsider making a snap judgment on the sanity of the unfortunate victim. After all, no one takes the time to research, design and develop a weapon, such as mind control machines, unless they intend to use it.

Mind Control and Sex Slaves

Without any doubt whatsoever, the most controversial aspect of the whole mind-control scenario is that relating to what has become known within conspiracy circles as sexual slavery.

Basically, the story goes like this: within the worlds of government, the military and the intelligence community, there are powerful men who – lacking souls and consciences – have at their disposal numerous mind-controlled victims who they exploit for sex.

Rather like flesh-and-blood versions of *The Stepford Wives*, many are almost zombie-like in nature when under the influence of their hypnotic-controllers, and they are virtual prisoners and slaves to the higher echelons of the world of government.

There have been numerous allegations made about shocking sexual abuse committed by famous figures in the political arena, as well as the means by which such sexual slaves were ensnared, hypnotically manipulated and used, and had their lives torn apart and destroyed. But is it really feasible that young, attractive women may have been exploited by dark and shadowy characters to become their unwitting slaves? Yes.

After the end of WWII, the United States had received from former Nazi Germany material dealing with their research into mind control. This newly acquired knowledge of mind control techniques had come from their experiments on prisoners in concentration camps, in which, according to experts, they learned of the effects of the calculated use of torture, drugs, hypnotism, electroshock, and sleep deprivation on an individual personality.

According to some, the result was found to be a fragmenting of the personality into separate components which are unaware of one another, creating what is known today as "Multiple Personality Disorder," or by the more recent, clinically-accepted term, "Dissociative Identity Disorder." The individual personality components could then be programmed to perform certain tasks, much like a computer. According to former FBI agent and mind control expert Ted Gunderson: "It's a combination of torture, hypnosis, drugs. And what happens is, they torture them so much, that their personality splits in order to endure the pain and misery. When their personality splits, they [become] another person, and it's through this technique that they train them." Such techniques could, says Gunderson, create Manchurian candidates, unwitting agents of espionage who could courier sensitive messages and even commit assassinations against their will, without any recollection of these events.

Indeed, according to many self-proclaimed victims of mind control, we are well ahead of the game today, and most say the CIA's motivation was never strictly "for the good of the country." For instance, consider the rumored existence of "Project MONARCH," the alleged offshoot of MK-ULTRA designed to create legions of so-called "mind-controlled sex slaves" for use by the rich and powerful. According to conspiracy theorist Fritz Springmeier, the project was called MONARCH after the butterfly of the same name. Training begins in early childhood, when, he says "Children who are traumatized have their legs tied and are electro-shocked and tortured until the alters (personalities) believe they are butterflies." The whole program is based on the "Marionette Programming" purportedly perfected in Nazi Germany with the same aim as MONARCH, in which sex slaves were created who believed themselves to be puppets ("marionettes") controlled by cruel masters.

The value of a mind-controlled sex slave is multi-faceted. For one thing, they can be used to satisfy the perversions of people in positions of power without jeopardizing that power, since a person under mind control is not likely to expose the event to public scrutiny. Furthermore, these encounters can be videotaped for the purpose of blackmailing public officials and businessmen should they at any time step out of line, or do anything to endanger the intelligence community's global plan. (Some people who purport the existence of Project MONARCH might also believe that the CIA is under the control of the Illuminati "New World Order" conspiracy of global domination.)

Then there is the financial aspect. A sex slave can be prostituted from childhood on to wealthy individuals who will pay large sums of money for the experience. They can also be used in child pornography to be sold on the global market. Many MONARCH "survivors" claim that unwanted, expendable sex slaves are picked to star in the most controversial pictures of all--snuff films, the existence of which has yet to be proven according to the FBI. The slaves are also, say the stories, used as drug mules for the CIA's secret trafficking of illegal substances.

The money derived from these black market transactions of drugs and sex is used, they say, to fund the CIA's many top secret and under-budgeted black operations, as well as to line the pockets of the perpetrators. Potential slaves are chosen for their genetic propensity for suggestibility, hypnotizability, dissociation, and high intelligence. In the past ten years or more, a number of these so-called "survivors" have "recovered" their memories and come forward about their past abuse at the hands of the government. Many have written books, such as Brice Taylor's *Thanks for the Memories: The Truth Has Set Me Free*, Annie McKenna's *Paperclip Dolls*, and Cathy O'Brien's *The TRANCE Formation of America*. Of these, Cathy O'Brien is perhaps the most well-known.

It's hard to think of a catchier opening line for a chapter than one that includes the words, "substituting his penis for my mother's nipple." Cathy couldn't think of a better one either as she described how her "pedophile" father, Earl O'Brien, allegedly first began to train her sexually. Cathy claims to have come from a family of multi-generational incest perpetrators, where daddy abused all of the kids, and all of the kids abused each other. Growing up in Muskegon, Michigan, a "pedophile capital," according to Cathy, it wasn't long before Cathy's father was whoring her around for use in lucrative child pornography. In time, Mr. O'Brien was caught, but instead of going to jail, he was visited, says Cathy, by future President Gerald Ford, who offered him a deal: sell Cathy into the MONARCH program, and receive immunity from prosecution. The CIA allegedly had good reason to seek Cathy out because, she says, "...they knew that any child that was sexually abused to that extent would be suffering from this dissociative disorder that they were interested in targeting for mind control."

And so her formal MONARCH training began. "Not long after that," she explains in her book, "my father was flown to Boston for a two-week course at Harvard on how to raise me for …Project MONARCH." From then on, Cathy was prostituted to a long list of high-ranking individuals, such as Michigan State Senator Guy VanderJagt, Canadian Prime Minister Pierre Trudeau, West Virginia Senator Robert Byrd (who later became her "owner" or "controller"), and the aforementioned Gerald Ford. She claims she was forced to engage in all sorts of strange perversions, from having sex with dogs to waving a small American flag with her rectum. This, coupled with her father's constant abuse and torture, kept her in a constant state of dissociation.

According to Cathy, she was controlled with form of Neuro-Linguistic Programming used on many MONARCH slaves, which involved the use of themes from *Wizard of Oz*, and various Disney children's films. She was taught to go into another dimension "over the rainbow" whenever the pain of the abuse became too much to bear, and to identify with Cinderella when her father assigned her a strict daily regimen of household chores, which was part of her slave programming. The hallucinogenic and multi-dimensional themes of *Alice in Wonderland* were also quite extensively used. This was done, not just to Cathy, but to all her brothers and sisters as well, who were also being used in the program. As she writes in her book, "My brother, now 37, remains psychologically locked into those traumatic childhood years and is obsessed with Disney themes and productions to this day. His house is decorated in Disney memorabilia, he wears Disney clothes, listens to my father's instructions on a Disney telephone, and maintains "When You Wish Upon a Star" as his favorite song, which has locked his children into the same theme."

Interestingly, the Disney programming claim is one made by almost every "recovered" MONARCH slave, although it's difficult to determine whether these claims began to surface before or after the publication of Cathy's book. For example, a number of them say that they were taken to Tinker Air Force Base in Oklahoma, where they were placed in electrified "Tinkerbell" cages, and tortured into creating child alters that would, like Peter Pan, never grow up.

However, Cathy did grow up, and although supposedly subjected to daily sexual abuse and torture, she managed to maintain an "A" average throughout her scholastic career, "because when trauma occurs that's too horrible to comprehend," says Cathy, "the brain automatically goes into its own mode, and photographically records events surrounding the trauma ... Since I was being traumatized all the time, I was photographically recording what I was being taught in school. So I got excellent grades." Throughout her childhood, she was isolated from society and popular culture, with the exception of the Disney movies previously mentioned, and was heavily exposed to country music. According to Cathy, the country music scene is heavily infiltrated by MONARCH operatives, because the tours they travel in throughout North America easily facilitate the trade of slaves and drugs.

When Cathy got older, she was married off by "The Company" to Wayne Cox, who fathered her daughter, Kelly (also a mind-controlled sex slave.) Later, she was married a second time to country music MC Alex Houston. Concurrently, she was also symbolically married to Senator Robert Byrd, who became her "controller," and largely dictated the events of her life from then on. She was sent to a sex slave training camp called "Charm School," directed, she says, by Pennsylvania Governor Dick Thornburgh and Ohio State Representative James Traficant [now in prison for bribery and racketeering]. After she graduated, Cathy says, she became a so-called "Presidential

Model," and was used to satisfy the sadistic sexual needs of executive-level members of government. From that point forward, the "Who's Who" list of johns she allegedly serviced became exponentially more impressive. She says she was nearly choked to death a number of times by Dick Cheney's enormous penis, and was violently raped by both Cheney and George Bush Sr., after being chased through the woods in a form of human hunting called "The Most Dangerous Game." She claims to have serviced both Bill and Hillary Clinton while the former was still Governor of Arkansas. She says she drove Hillary into a fit of ecstasy with the "Witch's Face" that her handlers had carved into her vagina which, says Cathy, "can give men pleasure," much like ribbed condoms do for women.

Cathy even claims that *Hustler*'s Larry Flynt was part of the conspiracy, and that he hired a photographer named Jimmy Walker to take pornographic pictures of her wedding night with Alex Houston, then had the photos published in one of his magazines. Writes Cathy, "Flynt was unequivocally the official White House Pornographer. [He] maintained … New World Order colleagues such as Presidents Reagan, Bush, and Ford, CIA Director Bill Casey, U.N. Ambassador Madeleine Albright, Senators Byrd and Spector, Congressmen Traficant and VanderJagt, Governors Thornburgh, Blanchard, and Alexander, and various world leaders such as Prime Minister of Canada Mulroney, President of Mexico de la Madrid, and Saudi Arabian King Fahd … to name a few." All of these people, by the way, are on Cathy's list of sexual assailants as well.

And another thing. Cathy O'Brien (like Brice Taylor, and a number of other proclaimed "Presidential Models") says that none of these high-ranking rapists ever used a condom, because both they and the Presidential Models had been inoculated against all sexually transmitted diseases. Says Cathy, "there was quite a bit of confidence surrounding the fact, and it was a known fact, that since I was used on a White House/Pentagon level…they would not get AIDS from me, because I was 'clean.' That was the term used."

And what was it that Gary Condit reportedly said to Torrie Hendley? "There's a cure for AIDS, anyway."

One of the consistencies that runs through almost all of the personal testimonies of the self-proclaimed MONARCH victims is the use of the occult and Satanism as a "trauma base." Cathy O'Brien vividly describes the "Rite to Remain Silent" she claims she endured at St. Francis of Assisi Church in Muskegon, a reversal of the Catholic mass in which she was allegedly doused in the blood of a freshly-slaughtered lamb and made to take an oath of secrecy. She also claims to have witnessed human sacrifices at Bohemian Grove retreat, an exclusive retreat for global movers and shakers, who meet on a private island every year in secret. They dress up in bizarre costumes and indulge in their most extreme perversions with mind-controlled "Stepford Whores," much like scenes from the Stanley Kubrick film *Eyes Wide Shut.*

Brice Taylor, who claims to have bedded down every President except since John Kennedy (except Carter and Nixon), also says that she experienced similar rituals throughout her abuse, including those involving human sacrifices, anti-Christian night services at Christian churches, being buried alive in a coffin, and being hung upon a cross. Annie McKenna has recovered numerous memories, she says, of her MONARCH-trained family donning dark hoods, chanting, and performing strange rites in graveyards.

Mind Stalkers

Even her own children, the first of which she had at age 11, were sacrificed to the blood cult. Writes McKenna, "The ritual abuse served two purposes. First, it exposed a child to horrific trauma, which caused the child to dissociate and create alters. Secondly, the belief was that if we ever did remember, the ritual abuse memories would surface first, and the medical community and public would label us insane."

The claims of mind control and MONARCH programming are just the latest details to be grafted onto the tales of Satanic Ritual Abuse (or SRA) that began to surface in the early 1980s. Although now largely discredited by the mental health establishment, SRA has long been a pervasive urban myth, if nothing more. Many groups, several of them affiliated with Protestant churches, believe in a large conspiracy of Satanists that spans the globe, and which controls the drug and child pornography industry (i.e., the Mafia), as well as, to the view of many, the government (i.e., the "Illuminati"). They believe that these people engage in the large-scale abduction and abuse of thousands of children for use in their sick, sadistic, Satanic sex rituals, and the pornographic documentation thereof. When not from "multi-generational Satanic families," like Taylor's and O'Brien's, where their parents willingly submit them to the MONARCH program, children are supposedly snatched off the streets--the familiar milk carton kids. According to the lore, the conspirators even infiltrate pre-schools and day care centers to access children there.

Ted Gunderson has personally investigated the famous McMartin Pre-School SRA case, even going so far as to hire an archeologist to dig for underground tunnels reported by the children. The children reported that in these tunnels they were subjected to sexual abuse, animal sacrifices, and Disney-based mind control programming by, among others, Steve Garvey, Chuck Norris, and Raymond Buckey, the school's owner. Gunderson claims, "we found the tunnels under the school. ... We found 2000 animal bones ..." Gunderson believes wholeheartedly that, "The Satanic cult movement dovetails with U.S. intelligence ... in addition to being involved in ... kidnapping, they were taking kids out of Boy's Town, and out of foster homes and orphanages, and flying them ... to Washington, D.C. for sex orgy parties with congressmen and senators. Barney Frank ... [has] been identified by the kids, and George Bush Sr. has been at the parties while he was Vice-President. ...[We're] talking about a large-scale pedophile ring, and a large-scale kidnapping ring ... known as "The Finders." It's a CIA covert operation running out of Washington, D.C. ... that's just a cover name for finding children..."

"The Finders" and Project MONARCH were implicated in Nebraska's "Franklin Cover-Up," also investigated by Gunderson, and by the author of *The Franklin Cover-Up*, former State Senator John DeCamp. In a civil case against 16 people, including Laurence E. King (manager of the failed Franklin Savings and Loan), Harold Anderson (publisher of the *Omaha World Herald*), and the Omaha Police Department, plaintiff Paul Bonacci was awarded $1 million by U.S. District Court Judge Warren Urbom in February 1999. In reference to King, the Judge found that he had "continually subjected the plaintiff to repeated sexual assault, false imprisonment, infliction of extreme emotional distress, organized and directed Satanic rituals, forced the plaintiff to 'scavenge' for children to be part of the defendant King's sexual abuse and pornography ring, forced the plaintiff to engage in numerous sexual contacts with the defendant King and others, and participate in deviant sexual games and masochistic orgies with minor children."

Mind Stalkers

Bonacci testified that he was flown on hundreds of trips to Washington, D.C., Kansas City, Chicago, Minnesota, and Los Angeles, where he was taken to "thousands" of pedophilic and sadomasochistic parties, drugged, and prostituted to the rich and powerful. Bonacci admits to participating in the kidnapping of then-12-year-old paper boy Johnny Gosch in Des Moines, Iowa, a story profiled extensively on *America's Most Wanted* and a number of other television programs. Johnny's mother, Noreen Gosch is convinced that Bonacci is telling the truth, and is also convinced that her son was kidnapped by joint intelligence-organized crime elements involved in Project MONARCH. Says Noreen, "[Bonacci] told us that he was put into MONARCH training at a very young age, right at Offutt Air Force Base... Johnny...was put through the same training..." In 1999, Johnny Gosch, a grown man at that point, came to visit his mother for a brief, covert visit in the middle of the night. "He told me that he had been subjected to mind control... and that his job was to compromise politicians, and any VIP that they felt they wanted to do that to... He only mentioned the Satanic rituals briefly."

One of the accused perpetrators who has been implicated by Noreen Gosch, Paul Bonacci, Cathy O'Brien, and a host of other "MONARCH victims" is Lt. Col. Michael Aquino, a former Green Beret and senior U.S. military intelligence officer once involved in the study of "PSY-OPS," or psychological warfare. He wrote an extensive essay with Colonel Paul E. Vallely (a Fox News Channel analyst) called "From PSY-OP to MindWar: The Psychology of Victory." In this essay, the authors advocated the use of propaganda, subliminal messages, air ionization, and ELF waves (i.e., putting low frequency signals in TV and radio broadcasts to induce specific states of mind) in times of war, both domestically and abroad, in order to manipulate public opinion of the war. Another interesting fact about Micheal Aquino: He just happens to be the leader and founder of the Temple of Set, a splinter group of the Church of Satan, in which Aquino was once a high-ranking member. The Temple of Set now has a number of chapters that operate on military bases. Interestingly, this group's rituals often involve Nazi symbols and rhetoric, and Aquino once performed a Satanic "working" at Heinrich Himmler's castle of Wewelsburg while in Germany on "official NATO business."

Predictably, this has caused no shortage of controversy to surround Michael Aquino. In the late 1980s, a Satanic Ritual Abuse/Child Sexual Abuse scandal broke out at a day care center on the Presidio military base in San Francisco, where Aquino was stationed. The children identified Aquino, as well as a Baptist Minister named Gary Hambright, who was indicted but not convicted. These kids claimed that the people who molested them were part of a "devil worship club," and were able to describe the inside of Aquino's house, where the abuse was said to have taken place. Other children identified Aquino by his nickname, "Mikey," although Anton LaVey. claims that Aquino's nickname was actually "Mickey" because his peculiar haircut made him look like Mickey Mouse (yet another Disney connection.)

Although Aquino was never indicted, and the charges against Hambright were dropped, several of the children contracted STDs, proving that someone had abused them. Later, after Hambright died of AIDS, the U.S. Army wrote to the children's parents urging them to get their children tested for HIV. They also paid a multi-million-dollar settlement to the victims. Furthermore, Aquino was "Titled" by the U.S. Army for "indecent acts with a child, sodomy, conspiracy, kidnapping, and false swearing," which

Mind Stalkers

means that they had probable cause to believe the offenses had been committed. According to many, the incident at Presidio was an outgrowth of Project MONARCH, and these people believe Aquino to be integrally involved in the program.

Paul Bonacci has identified Aquino as the one who ordered the kidnapping of Johnny Gosch, and says that Aquino had a "ranch" in Colorado that was a "safe house" for kidnapped children. Rusty Nelson, a photographer for the Franklin Cover-Up's, Lawrence King, and a convicted child pornographer, testified before a U.S. District Court on February 5, 1999 that he witnessed a suitcase full of cash being handed over to by King to Aquino that was "earmarked for the Nicaraguan Contras." Also, a number of mind-controlled sex slaves, including Cathy O'Brien, have listed Aquino as one of their "handlers." However, when I questioned Aquino about these allegations, he responded: "Throughout my entire career as an Army officer (1968-94), I never encountered any evidence of anything named or resembling 'Project MONARCH', never participated in anything involving children [or adult] 'sex slaves', never abused any children under any circumstances whatever, and never had any contact with any of the cranks who've thrown my name around with 'MONARCH.'"

The charges against Aquino perhaps lose credibility when we consider that many of the people who have made these claims have also implicated a so-called "Michael LaVey," who they say is a son of Anton LaVey. Noreen Gosch says that Michael LaVey was interviewed on a 20/20 special about her son's kidnapping, during which, according to her, "[Michael] LaVey said that he had been with Johnny on many occasions at the Satanic ritual ceremonies, where they serviced different men for their owners." Unfortunately for Noreen, no independent confirmation has surfaced that Anton had any son by that name. The late Anton LaVey. himself has been implicated as a Project MONARCH participant by a handful of people, such as Noreen Gosch, but not in any specific way. However, it is interesting to note that Anton LaVey. did consider Disneyland to be one of the happiest places on Earth, and his daughter Zeena LaVey. listed the 1950s thriller *The Most Dangerous Game.* as her favorite movie.

The process of deprogramming a presumed victim of Project MONARCH--identifiable by abnormally wide eyes (from the electroshock), odd-looking facial moles (caused by stun guns), a plastic smile, and generally robotic behavior--is a strange and controversial one. Since slaves are programmed to self-destruct if they should ever find themselves talking about their memories, therapists wishing to override these programs must be armed with the corresponding "deactivation codes." Mark Phillips, who "rescued" Cathy O'Brien from mind control, and co-authored *The TRANCE Formation of America.*, describes the process of deprogramming her: "I had to know certain codes, keys and triggers. I *had* to, and I was provided a few of those," by he says, covert communications from friends in the intelligence community. Thereafter, Cathy began to recover memories through extensive journal-writing practices. Brice Taylor used a collage method with pictures cut out of magazines.

Others use the more dubious methods of hypnosis, and similar New Age techniques to unlock memories supposedly repressed with programmed amnesia. Ritual trauma hypno-therapists such as D.C. Hammond, PhD., and Pamela J. Monday, PhD report discovering complex, multi-layered systems of programming that even take geometric shapes, such as pentagrams, hexagrams, or the cabalistic Tree of Life, complete with internal "landscapes" that have "mountains," "castles," and the like. They have found that some programs are guarded by "gatekeepers" with gothic, diabolical-sounding names, and different letters of programming are coded with letters from the Greek alphabet. For instance, Alpha is general programming, Beta involves sexual programming, Delta programming holds instructions for how to kill during ceremonies, Theta includes "psychic killing," and Omega involves suicidal, "self-destruct" programming, as well as self-mutilation. Zeta programming is related to the production of snuff films, and Omicron has to do with drug smuggling.

However, many mental health professionals cast doubt on the techniques used by hypno-therapists, charging that such practices create rather than recover memories, and so do the people who are accused of such heinous crimes on the evidence of the allged victim's "recovered memories." The accused are backed by an organization called The False Memory Syndrome Foundation, whose spokesperson, Pamela Freyd, questions the motives of those who are, "using hypnosis, guided imagery, sodium amytal, relaxation exercise, participation in groups, reading suggestive literature and other techniques in an effort to excavate memories," Freyd explains. "Although people may remember things with any of these techniques, there is absolutely no evidence that what they remember is historically accurate." She also questions the validity of multiple personalities in general, stating that, "Many in the psychiatric community believe that MPD is iatrogenic, that is, caused by the use of hypnosis and the type of interviewing techniques of the doctor."

Confirming the validity of another person's memory is nearly impossible, especially if every other person involved in the memory denies that it took place. However, it may perhaps be unfair to label as "impossible" or "ridiculous" the memories of other people which merely lie beyond the spectrum of our own experience. Many of us received religious indoctrination from our family as we grew up, and were forced to participate in weird ceremonies that made us uncomfortable. Isn't it logical that if our parents were Satanists or occultists, they might subject us to similar indoctrination? And since Satanic and occult practices purportedly bestow worldly power upon their practitioners, isn't it logical that some of our most powerful leaders might participate in such practices? Isn't it logical that they would make use of occult-based mind control techniques such as hypnotism, rituals, mind-altering drugs, and Neuro-Linguistic Programming (i.e., rote memorization of "magic words")--techniques that have been traditional components of religious ceremonies, from the mystical priesthoods of Babylon, Greece, Rome and Egypt to the "cults" of today?

The CIA's interest in mind control is well-documented, and there was certainly a time, in which they had no compunction about subjecting unwitting subjects to experiments that might harm them, or which might go against their intended will. The idea that the CIA would traffic in guns, drugs and other contraband in order to fund their secret projects is becoming more generally accepted, especially after *The San Francisco Chronicle*'s Gary Webb. investigated the funding of Contra aid in 1996.

Furthermore, we know that men in positions of power often require a greater-than-average number of sexual partners, often choosing extremely young women (or men), sometimes prostitutes, to satisfy their often kinky desires. Perhaps this is just a result of the greater-than-average testosterone levels often found in aggressive power-seekers. That the CIA would supply these prostitutes in exchange for their much-needed

Mind Stalkers

Black Ops funding, and that they would keep these prostitutes mind-controlled into silence using the above-mentioned techniques, so as to cover their own tracks, may not be impossible to believe.

Perhaps what people do find unbelievable is the sheer sensationalism of so many of the "Project MONARCH" stories. The mental picture of George Bush, Sr. sodomizing a seven-year-old boy, or of Bill Clinton participating in cannibalistic baby sacrifice, is not one that most people can take seriously. Even more difficult to overcome, perhaps, is a natural disbelief that arises when a person claiming to have been under complete mental robotism, and subjected to unimaginable torture throughout his or her entire life appears to "recover" so quickly after the "memories" are revealed during therapy. Some of them even go on to write books, conduct seminars, and make radio appearances, becoming a professional victim-expert. Perhaps we will never know who is and who isn't telling the truth about MONARCH mind control--unless the documents that supposedly exist are one day declassified. However, the tales of Project MONARCH provide an interesting framework in which to interpret current events, especially the never-ending sex scandals that perpetually crop up amongst our public figures.

Mind Stalkers

For our FREE catalog of books, DVDS, audio CDs, and other mind-blowing items. Send your name and address to:

**Global Communications
P.O. Box 753
New Brunswick, NJ 08903**

**You can also send us an email at:
mrufo8@hotmail.com**

Visit our website at: www.conspiracyjournal.com

Printed in Great Britain
by Amazon